CLASSROOM POWER RELATIONS

Understanding Student–Teacher Interaction

೮ಾ ◆ ೮ಐ

CLASSROOM POWER RELATIONS

Understanding Student–Teacher Interaction

ca   ◆   ca

Mary Phillips Manke
Mankato State University

LEA LAWRENCE ERLBAUM ASSOCIATES, PUBLISHERS
1997 Mahwah, New Jersey   London

Lawrence Erlbaum Associates, Inc., Publishers
10 Industrial Avenue
Mahwah, New Jersey 07430

Library of Congress Cataloging-in-Publication Data

Manke, Mary Phillips.
Classroom power relations : understanding student–teacher interaction / Mary Phillips Manke.
p.   cm.
Includes bibliographical references and index.
ISBN 0-8058-2496-0 (pbk. : alk. paper)
1. Teacher–student relationships—United States—Case studies.   2. Interaction analysis in education—United States—Case studies.   3. Classroom environment—United States—Case studies. I. Title.
LB1033.M2123   1997   97-12619
371.102'3—dc21   CIP

Books published by Lawrence Erlbaum Associates are printed on acid-free paper, and their bindings are chosen for strength and durability.

Printed in the United States of America
10 9 8 7 6 5 4 3 2

Contents

ℰ☧ ◆ ℭ

PART II: TEACHERS AND STUDENTS CONSTRUCTING POWER RELATIONS

                One Aspect of Classroom Power Relations

Chapter 6   *"Sally, Would You Like to Sit Down?" How*   75
                Teachers Use Politeness and Indirect Discourse

Chapter 7   *Defining Classroom Knowledge: The Part*   92
                That Students Play

Chapter 8   *Students in Conflict With Teachers' Agendas:*   106
                Interactive Contributions to Classroom Power
                Relations

Chapter 9   *How Is It Useful to Look at Classrooms*   126
                in This Way?

Appendix: *Exploring Ideas About Power Relations*   140
                in Classrooms

                References   164

                Author Index   167

                Subject Index   169

Preface

⁊   ♦   ⁋

This book is written for teachers, future teachers, and teacher educators, in the hope that it will be useful to them as they consider how students and teachers together construct their lives in classrooms.

Based on an ethnographic study of three elementary classrooms, the book reflects my understanding and interpretation of power relations as I observed them. It is centered on a constructivist view of power relations, not as brought into classrooms from the outside world, by the teacher or anyone else, but as created inside classrooms through the actions of teachers and students that take place every day.

As I worked with the data I had collected and as I applied the concepts I was developing to thinking about my own teaching, I understood more clearly the potential usefulness of the view of power relations I was forming. In every classroom, whether or not the teacher is trying to share power, control, or authority with the students, students participate with teachers in developing the classroom's power relations—the set of local rules that determines what teachers and students can actually do in that classroom. In a political world in which teachers are constantly held responsible for every outcome of classroom life, this concept has promise for helping teachers perceive their classrooms as places in which they and the students are working together, and are jointly responsible for outcomes. This realistic basis for understanding classroom life can be helpful to teachers, and perhaps reduce some of the stress that comes from taking sole responsibility for what happens in their classrooms.

HOW THIS BOOK IS ORGANIZED

The contents of this book are divided into nine chapters: an introduction, three narrative chapters, four chapters of analysis, and a conclusion. The first chapter offers a brief introduction to the concept of power relations used throughout the book. It traces this concept to four sources: my own experience as a parent and teacher, a developing metaphor for power relations that envisions teachers and students constructing a building called "What Teachers and Students Can Do Here," some sources in educational literature, and the ethnographic data from my study of three elementary classrooms. The chapter closes with a review of the research processes used in collecting that data.

The next three chapters are collected into Part 1, Narratives of Classroom Life. Each chapter is devoted to one of the three classrooms. They provide a context in which the reader is prepared for the analysis to follow, as well as a basis for discussion and comparison to other classrooms. A description of the community, the school, and the classroom day is followed by a narrative account of a portion of a typical or sample day. In each case, this narrative was developed from the ethnographic data. Chapter 2 describes Sunny Kaminski's semirural first-grade classroom, where a whole-language teacher offered children many choices within her framework of expectations. Chapter 3 tells about Aileen Corvo's classroom, an urban fifth grade. This teacher had an authoritarian style; the chapter features instances of student compliance and student resistance. Chapter 4 is set in Sue Anderson's classroom. In this suburban fifth grade the teacher focused on student participation in classroom goal setting and on what she described as sharing control with students.

The next four chapters form Part 2, Teachers and Students Constructing Power Relations. Each chapter considers one of the four broad categories of interaction that were developed from the data. Although there is a great deal of overlapping ideas among the four areas, separating them permits easier discussion of themes and patterns. Chapters 5 and 6 focus primarily on the actions of teachers; chapter 5 centers on teacher organization of time and space, the area in which teachers act out of sight of the students. Chapter 6, titled "'Sally, Would You Like to Sit Down?' How Teachers Use Politeness and Indirect Discourse" describes how teachers use politeness formulas and indirect discourse, and how students sometimes make this impossible. Chapters 7 and 8 center on students' contributions to classroom power relations. Chapter 7 focuses on how students and teachers together define what will count as classroom knowledge; chapter 8 looks closely at students opposing teacher agendas.

The final chapter offers suggestions about the role ideas explored in this book can play in shaping teachers' classroom practice. It asks the question, "How does it help to look at classrooms in this way?" It outlines benefits for teachers in recognizing that classroom power relationships are not the teacher's sole responsibility, that giving children choices is not the same as abdicating power, and that the choices teachers make about classroom management are based on their beliefs about teaching and learning.

Following chapter 9, an annotated bibliography provides guidance for those wishing to explore the literature of power relations, classroom inter-action, and the methodological tools used to understand the data used for this book.

ACKNOWLEDGMENTS

My gratitude to the teachers whose names in this book are Sunny Kaminski, Aileen Corvo, Courtney Bridgestone, and Sue Anderson. Your willingness to welcome me, my notebook, and my video camera into your classrooms, answer my many questions, share your thoughts and reflections, and allow me to write about you was a wonderful gift. Without your generosity, this book would never have been started. Also, thanks to the principals who accepted my assurances that my work would not harm their schools and to the children, whose friendly responses made my work a pleasure.

My appreciation to all the critics of various parts of this book. The thoughts shared by the excellent reviewers provided by Lawrence Erlbaum Associates, Kathy Bickmore (University of Toronto), Patricia A. Gross (Ursinus College), and Celia Oyler (Syracuse University), were essential in shaping the book and refining its focus. They, of course, are not responsible for what I have written, but their thought-provoking comments have helped me in many ways. I also want to thank the reviewers from Division G of the American Educational Research Association (AERA) who commented on earlier drafts of chapters 5, 6, and 7, as well as the respondents and session participants when I presented each of those chapters at AERA. Your comments were written down, remembered, and used.

Thanks also to Eric Bredo, Robert Covert, Robert McNergney, Peter Hackett, and Ellen Contini-Morava, who were the members of my disser-tation committee at the University of Virginia. Eric pushed me to clarify a theoretical understanding of power relations; Bob Covert encouraged and enlightened my journey into qualitative research; Bob McNergney gave me access to the first classroom I studied, offered me both personal and professional support, and asked many provocative questions; Pete was unendingly supportive in every way over the 14 years from my first class in the master's program to the day my dissertation was accepted; and Ellen guided me in learning about the role of discourse and never failed to point out and help me correct my confusion and imprecision. I extend my most sincere gratitude to each of them.

Three other faculty members at the University of Virginia were also essential to my life and learning there; sadly, none of them is alive to receive my thanks. They are Mary Catherine Ellwein, Brenda Loyd, and Dell Hymes.

I would like to acknowledge the strong influence that Ray McDermott of Stanford University has had on the contents of this book. From the classes I had with him and from his writings, I learned an approach to ethnography and to understanding human interaction that has remained central to my thinking. I have cited his work often and with the greatest respect.

My appreciation also to Naomi Silverman, the editor of this book, whose support has been so helpful in bringing this project to completion. Her ability to see, not just a problem, but what was causing it and how it could be solved, was invaluable.

Last, a special thank you to Celia Oyler. I have appreciated her respect for my work, her thoughtful and specific suggestions for improving it, and her willingness to encourage me when I was ready to give up. Her own work has been clarifying and inspirational for me, but her friendship has been the best gift of all.

—*Mary Phillips Manke*

Chapter 1

Introduction

ഇ ◆ Ზ

Who has power in classrooms? Most people would say it is the teacher who has power. Willard Waller, an early sociologist of education, wrote in 1932, "Children are certainly defenseless against the machinery with which the adult world is able to enforce its decisions: the result of the battle [between teachers and students] is foreordained" (p. 196).

Waller's statement expresses the understanding of classroom power that prevails for most people—teachers, administrators, educational researchers—in our culture. It is an understanding that focuses on opposition between teachers and students as well as one that assigns power to the teacher alone.

In this book, you will read about a much more complex conception of classroom power. It portrays students and teachers in power relationships they build together and calls into question common assumptions about the workings and results of power in the classroom.

Underlying Waller's statement is this belief: *The teacher must have the power in the classroom.* Let us work out some of what this belief implies. First, it seems to mean that power is something you can have, an object that a person can own. In this book, the understanding of power is quite different: Power is a structure of relationships—a structure in which teachers and students can build or participate. Power is not an object and cannot be owned by anyone. The structure of relationships is called power because it, rather than the individuals who create it, is what shapes people's actions.

1

Second, Waller's idea implies that the teacher is the only one who "has" power. If this were the case, the teacher would also be the only person responsible for what happens in the classroom. Every student action, every bit of student learning, every aspect of classroom activity would be under the teacher's control; therefore, the teacher would be accountable for every outcome. What a crushing burden of responsibility for a teacher to bear! Yet, this level of responsibility is implied by the statement, "The teacher must have the power in the classroom".

Teachers naturally look for ways to escape from this burden, but most of these have some negative results. One possibility is to claim that the teacher's power is overwhelmed by social and political forces outside the classroom—forces out of the teacher's control. A teacher who tries to limit his or her responsibility by making this claim may, ironically, feel powerless, and give up trying. Another possible approach is to label some students as having disabilities or defects that are not subject to the teacher's control; this has led to unnecessary exclusion and devaluing of these students.

Third, Waller's idea indicates that power cannot be shared. The teacher owns power, and if the teacher does not own it, it has been lost. For Waller, if teachers do not win the "battle" he describes, they cannot be teachers. Such a belief requires teachers to focus their attention on keeping ownership of classroom power, often to the detriment of their focus on the needs of students and on the learning.

This book makes the claim that teachers are not the sole owners of classroom power. Instead, it proposes that teachers and students, like any group of participants in a particular context, are jointly responsible for constructing power in the classroom. The teacher is not solely responsible, but instead bears a share of the responsibility for classroom events and outcomes; students make their own contributions, influencing both their own actions and those of the teacher. Understanding power as a matter of relationships implies that power in the classroom cannot be constructed by the teacher alone. How can one individual build relationships? They must be the work of all who participate—both teachers and students.

Our culture envisions classrooms like those Waller describes, in which teachers have power and students do not. This understanding is part of the cultural knowledge that students and teachers bring to school. Unexamined because it is so pervasive, this vision of classrooms permeates the institutional arrangements of schools. For example, teachers are seen as problems if they do not seem to have power—to be in control of their students. Such teachers are more likely to receive assistance or even to be dismissed than teachers whose students do not learn.

The school provides support for teachers in controlling student actions. Students are sent to the office to be punished or scolded by administrators or secretaries; they stand in hallways and receive public disapproval; they serve detentions; they are suspended; in some schools, they receive corporal punishment. Their parents are not surprised to be asked to support the school's discipline. Also, schools support methods of instruction and assessment based on teacher power and student acquiescence. These include lecture-and-recitation methods of instruction and testing as a method of evaluation.

Because "everyone knows" that teachers have power, not only are many of our practical ideas about classrooms, students, and teachers based on this "general knowledge," but its implications affect many areas of educational thought (Hustler & Payne, 1982). For example, process–product research about teaching assumes it is what the teacher does that decides what will happen in the classroom, and this assumption has shaped the effective schools movement (Carlsen, 1991). It also permeates classroom management literature, whose purpose is to instruct teachers in those competencies that will make them victors in the battle described by Waller (e.g., Cangelosi, 1988; Duke, 1982; Swick, 1985). Behavioral measures of teacher competency that judge teachers by observing whether or not students are on task and whether direct teacher intervention is necessary to keep them on task, are founded on this same assumption (Morine-Dershimer, 1985). When teachers are criticized for accepting low student effort in exchange for compliance (Sizer, 1984; Sedlak, Wheeler, Pullin, & Cusick, 1986), it is assumed that they have relinquished their power over students.

Because this traditional view of classroom power relationships is so widespread, a shift to an understanding of classroom power as jointly constructed, and therefore shared, calls for significant changes in how we think about many aspects of schooling.

SOURCES OF THIS CONCEPT OF POWER

The idea of power is a familiar one, rich in both political and personal associations. In considering it, I have felt surrounded by varied memories and connections. Here, I want to talk about four different kinds of thinking that underlie the concept of classroom power that I explore in this book. The first is my own experience—as a teacher and a parent—with power and my reflections on this experience. The second is a metaphor of power relationships; the development of this metaphor has been crucial in the growth of my understanding of this constructivist concept of classroom power. The third source is the literature about the concept of power and about classroom interaction. The fourth source is the ethnographic data, collected in three classrooms over a 5-year period, that pushed me to new efforts at understanding how classroom power relations work.

Conflicts in the Arena of Power: Parenting and Teaching

As I began to work with the idea of power, I recognized that this concept has many negative connotations for me. I shy away from the notion of power, as I do from concepts of control, authority, discipline, management, boss, tyranny, even fascism; I am much more attracted to ideas like liberty, freedom, choice, consensus, equality, and democracy. I seek to center my life around the second list and often feel angry, imposed on, or even guilty when I encounter the first. Reaching adulthood in the 1960s, I am part of a generation that valued, or claimed to value, freedom more than power.

Yet, I cannot deny that power is part of my life, of every life. I am subject to the authority, control, discipline, and management of others in many settings. As a parent, as a teacher, as a member of various groups, as an advocate of various causes, I am drawn into situations in which I am powerful or in control. I feel considerable conflict when I recognize that this is happening.

As a single parent of four children (now all adults), I intended to maintain a democratic family, participate in shared decision making, and avoid seeming to be a tyrant to my children. Yet, this often did not seem possible. I needed to protect myself from my children's demands on my time, my emotions, and my other resources. I was the one with the checks, the credit card, the car; often my "Yes" or "No" had a very different weight from theirs. Also, as an adult, I felt responsible for them; I had knowledge of the world and a concern for the future that they lacked. Looking back, I can see my life with my children as an endless conflict among my own values, centered around the issue of power.

As a classroom teacher for 11 years, in preschool and kindergarten, I again found myself in a quandary as to my own power. I did not want to see myself as a powerful teacher, but as friend and helper to "my kids"—my students. Yet, principals, fellow teachers, and, indeed, I had definite expectations that children would act in prescribed ways. Because all of us were enmeshed in our culture's understanding of classroom power, it was expected by all that I would have the ability to see that they did.

We expected that these young children would not hurt one another (or their teachers). They would cooperate about matters such as moving from one room to another, using the bathrooms without supervision, and eating and resting with others. When activities were over, they would clean up after themselves. When group activities were planned, they would pay attention and not interfere with others. Also, we expected that they would participate in activities through which they would learn.

Because I was so uncomfortable with the idea of being powerful in the classroom, I naturally moved as much of my power as possible into indirect and invisible modes. If there were things that children had to do, those things would be so well-planned and so much fun that they would want to do them. Learning activities would involve many choices among good alternatives; children would feel that they were choosing what to do. Group activities like reading aloud and singing would be so interesting, so well-done, that they would keep the children's attention without coercion. If children had to clean up, routines would be established, advance warnings given, and storage systems simplified to ease their tasks. Most of all, I would always speak politely and gently—even while telling children what to do.

Mine was a fairly conscious effort to move classroom management into the realm of indirection and invisibility. It was not an unusual effort. Pick up any issue of the National Association for the Education of Young Children's journal, *Young Children*, and you will find articles explaining how to manage children without seeming to coerce them. Usually, my effort was highly effective. Well-organized, happy classrooms were my trademark for years.

However, the last year I taught, before graduate school, was a hard one. I worked with a group of children who were less than willing to let my invisible power work on them. Several had been in school together for the previous 1-1/2 years, and they had some highly effective moves of their own in the arena of power. If it was not quite true to say that they coordinated their efforts, it was certainly true that their timing was skillful. I redoubled my efforts to control them and to keep my control invisible; they were still successful in bringing issues to the surface. They forced me to recognize that my good early childhood teacher moves were really power moves. This reality had briefly surfaced before that year; now I could not ignore it.

When I began this research and worked on ideas of power, I needed to be aware of my discomfort with traditional notions of power. Finding in the ethnographic data those incidents that could be understood as the basis for a nontraditional grounded theory about power, I had to repeatedly ask myself whether or not my aversion to the traditional theory was shaping my thinking in ways that I did not suspect. I could not doubt that the conflicts I experienced as a parent and teacher were one root of my thinking, as I stripped the concept of power of many of its old associations and relocated it in the arena of interaction, of relationship.

Yet, in reflecting on my past experiences, I saw that they might be better explained by the theory of power I was developing rather than by traditional notions. The question was not, as I had felt, one of whether I had power or gave it up. Rather it was one of how my children and I, or my young students and I, constructed together the power relationships within which we lived. Some of my discomfort with memories of past times evaporated as I began to have a better understanding of the ideas I was developing.

A Metaphor of Power Relationships

The metaphors we use in understanding our experiences can often have important effects in shaping that understanding (Lakoff & Johnson, 1980). Traditional metaphors for power in classrooms have named the teacher as autocratic ruler, drill sergeant, factory manager, leader in battle; students have been called subjects, recruits, laborers, soldiers. The metaphor I am proposing is quite different from those. It is more like the conceptions of power developed by Foucault and Janeway, with their metaphors of web and seesaw. According to Foucault (1980), "Power is employed and exercised through a net-like organization. And not only do individuals circulate between its threads; they are always in the position of simultaneously undergoing and exercising this power" (p. 98).

Janeway's conception of power is as follows:

[Power's] being is becoming. Its steady existence [is] derive[d] from ceaseless shifts and tensions, its balance is maintained by thrust and response, hope and frustration, and by the practical actions that grow out of compromises and confrontations among its myriad human components. (1980, p. 3)

The metaphor I have used is one of building a physical structure; the process of developing and extending this metaphor has shaped and expressed my thinking about teachers and students interacting in classrooms. I imagine students and teachers as building rooms or spaces in which they can act independently or influence the actions of others, building areas off to the side of the main structure where they can live and work without conflict with others, and sometimes seeking to build in areas where their plans and actions conflict with those of other members.

The name of the structure that students and teachers build in the interactional space they live in is "What Teachers and Students Can Do Here." Its name implies its function; in it, classroom power resides. The bricks and planks, and girders and beams of this structure are the actions of participants. There is an unlimited supply of such building materials, and unlimited (imaginary) space in which to build. All members can contribute to building the structure; there are no limits on the size or shape of the building. To the extent that there are plans for this improvised building, they are the agendas that students and teachers bring to or create within the classroom.

This structure has a strongly reflexive quality. It is made from actions of students and teachers, yet it also specifies the actions in which students and teachers may or may not engage. As they test and explore the structure's limits, they continue to build and remodel the structure itself. What teachers do shapes both their own future actions and student actions; what each student does limits both the actions of teachers and actions of other students. Each student makes an individual contribution to the building of the structure.

The actions that serve as the material of the structure are shaped by the individuality of each teacher and student. Each has a personality and point of view; each has needs to meet and a personal stock of information and experience. These, together with a combination of more or less shared cultural influences, shape the actions of each individual.

Some of the cultural influences shaping individual members are shared by several, many, most, or all members of the group. They have a broad influence on the structure that is created. Yet, this influence is actualized only through what individual members do and has no way of making a separate contribution to the building of power relationships.

This metaphor suggests the mutuality of the power relations of teacher and students, the extent to which they may at times agree, disagree, or be out of touch as to their goals, and the constant process of change and effort that is characteristic of classroom life.

Ideas From the Literature of Power and Interaction

At the end of this book, there is an annotated bibliography of a portion of this literature, which extends in time from ancient Greece to the present, and in subject matter from politics and military action to psychology, sociology, sociolinguistics, and history. In this section, I highlight four key ideas about classroom power—derived from the literature on power and interaction—that have significantly influenced the understanding of power discussed in this text:

1. Power belongs to both teacher and students. Just as teachers have interactional resources that affect how students act, students use their own resources to shape teachers' behavior.
2. Human interaction creates a context in which further interaction occurs. The actions of participants are shaped by the actions of those around them—both teachers and students.
3. Teachers and students bring their own agendas to the classroom—agendas with potential for significant conflict. For their own reasons, they often conceal these agendas beneath a public shared agenda of cooperation or perhaps beneath some other shared agenda.
4. Some of the resources teachers and students use as they build a structure of power relationships can be found in the area of discourse; teachers (and students) choose from an array of interactional resources as they construct classroom power relationships.

It was Harry Wolcott's (1987) article "The Teacher as Enemy" that first led me to reconsider the traditional notion of the teacher as the owner of power in the classroom. An anthropologist, Wolcott combined research with elementary school teaching in a Kwakiutl village in British Columbia. Painfully, he learned that his own image of himself as teacher was not that of his students.

Much like myself as a kindergarten teacher, Wolcott, as an elementary teacher, wanted his students to see him as mentor, friend, and leader; instead, they saw him as enemy. They were not really at war with him, he says, but acted like prisoners of war in a prison camp where he was the commander, and they were locked up together. He observed that his students were often physically, but not mentally, present in the classroom, focusing on home and family while being harangued by their teacher/commander. By cooperating with him, the students were "selling out, defecting, turning into traitors," like prisoners of war who have become trusties by betraying their own side (p. 147).

Wolcott's students expressed their hostility in words, often in their journals, but they showed it most strongly through their actions. They kept the pace of classroom activity slow, worked in groups, rather than individually as he expected, and ignored or completed assignments as they wished. They teased and bullied one another, yet protected one another from being seen as incompetent. They had their own expectations of what teachers should do and be, and they tried to influence Wolcott to meet them, using ignoring, misunderstanding, and interrupting as strategies.

Wolcott attributed much of the opposition he experienced to cultural differences between him and his students. What was more important in shaping my conceptualization of classroom power relationships was that he experienced his students as much more powerful than he—not merely as resisting his teacher power, but as overwhelming it.

McDermott and Roth's (1978) article "The Social Organization of Behavior: Interactional Approaches" was the source of a basic assumption of this work: When people communicate with one another they are conducting an interactive process through which they construct the context in which they communicate, in which they live together. Closely related to constructivist notions of cognitive interaction, this idea created a bridge in my thinking between ideas about power relationships and the wider realm of human communication. It implies that the construction of power relationships in the classroom must be a result of actions of all participants, and not of the teacher alone. For McDermott and Roth, "a person's behavior is best described in terms of the behavior of those immediately about that person, those with whom that person is doing interactional work in the construction of recognizable social scenes or events" (p. 321).

In a closed society like that of a classroom, "those immediately about that person" are the teacher (and perhaps other classroom adults) and the students.

For McDermott and Roth, who are microethnographers, specific actions in classrooms are the focus of study. Like them, I based my analysis of classroom interaction on what can be seen and heard in the classroom's defined and insular space. Influences from outside the classroom—large social forces, institutional forces, and the personal experiences and cultures of teachers and students—can only be seen as they have affected the actions of teachers and students. I believe another kind of research is required to uncover the influences that shaped the behaviors I saw and describe in this book.

Yet, it is important to at least acknowledge what is much harder to observe—the effects of the larger society on what occurs within the classroom. The interactive construction of power relationships and, indeed, of all aspects of life in the classroom, takes place within that society. The school, the community, and the nation surround the classroom and limit, as well as influence, what takes place within it.

These influences are felt through imposed curricula and institutional rules (Apple, 1993, 1996; Carnoy, 1984; Gore, 1995; Karabel & Halsey, 1977) and expressed expectations (Finn, 1972; McCormick & Noriega, 1986; Modzierz, McConville, & Strauss, 1968; Rist, 1970), yet they can be made real only through the actions and choices of students and teachers. However explicit these curricula, rules, and expectations are when the classroom door is shut, they are subject to negotiation within the power relations that the people in the classroom have constructed.

Less directly, these larger influences act through each individual in the classroom, because each has been shaped by them. From interactions in the larger society, as well as from those in the classroom, individuals learn patterns, possibilities, roles, and actions they will bring to the classroom. Students and teachers have their own needs to meet, and also their own stock of information and experience to guide them when they act. Some of these cultural or societal influences shaping individual students and teachers are shared by several, many, or all members of the group, and therefore, may seem to have a broader influence within the classroom.

What is important for myself, in this research, is to recognize that this influence is actualized only through individual members and their actions and has no avenue for making a separate contribution to the building of power relationships. Only when a teacher or student acts within the classroom can the influence of the larger society be seen; direct observation of its influence is impossible, and indirect observation of such influence must be extrapolated from what can be observed. This is why the consideration of such influences is not a focus of this book, which is based on data gathered from direct observation in the classroom.

McDermott and Tylbor's (1986) article "On the Necessity of Collusion in Conversation" was another key source of ideas. Their work clarified the idea of agendas or plans that shape the construction of power relationships. They speak of agreed-on, colluded-on agendas that cloak underlying and conflicting agendas of various participants in an interaction. These agreed-on agendas are known to all participants (though perhaps to some participants more clearly than others) to be "not what is really happening."

In the three classrooms where my ethnographic work took place—a first-grade class and two fifth-grade classes—it was clear that the teachers' agenda was to control student actions to facilitate student learning; students were seeking to act without the constraints of adult responsibility, seeking to "have an interesting day" (Fraatz, 1987, p. 31; the same idea appears in

Cazden, 1988). The shared, or colluded-on, agenda in the three classrooms I studied was one of cooperation (or social politeness), which often concealed conflicts between teacher and student agendas (Sedlak et al., 1986; Sizer, 1984; White, 1989). This could be phrased as the following: "we are here to cooperate with one another (in learning)" or perhaps "we are here to maintain positive social relations (while we learn)."

The teachers' agenda, as I saw it, came from our culture's understanding of what classrooms are supposed to be about: Teachers "have power"; they exercise control over students because they are responsible adults and because that control leads to student learning. Thus, teachers' contributions to the building of power relationships were usually actions intended to control students. Most of the time, they preferred to collude with the students on the public agenda of cooperation in order to smooth their path toward control of student actions.

The students' agenda arose from one aspect of our culture's view of what childhood is—a time of noncompliance, a time in which children find and develop spaces in their lives that are not under the control of adults. Children are expected to enjoy a kind of freedom not available to adults who have many responsibilities. (This notion surfaced as early as 1938, in an article by anthropologist Ruth Benedict, published in the journal *Psychiatry*.) Thus, the students had an agenda of maintaining their freedom of action. As Celia Oyler pointed out in her very helpful criticism of this book, it is possible for students to find that learning contributes to having an interesting day (Oyler, 1996), but an agenda of childhood as a time free from adult goals runs deep in our culture, and the resistance of young people to teacher agendas for learning can be strong.

Students sometimes found it in their interest to collude with the teacher in the public agenda of the classroom, the agenda of visible cooperation, thus creating more opportunities to act as they wished. At other times they tried to move the colluded-upon agenda into the open and confront it directly.

The three classrooms in this study were places where people usually spoke politely to one another, and appeared to cooperate in a common effort. Where extreme disruptions are common in classrooms (e.g., MacLaren, 1988), or where radically different educational goals are pursued (Swidler, 1979), teacher and student agendas, and especially the agreed-on agenda just described, might be different.

Elliot Mishler's (1972) "Implications of Teacher Strategies for Language and Cognition: Observations in First-grade Classrooms" was the source of the last key concept for this work. He identified verbal or discourse strategies teachers used to achieve various purposes. For example, one teacher he studied used language to establish herself as a coercive leader. She uttered threats to the group and characterized statements the children made as inappropriate or irrelevant, denying their claims to power. His analysis led me to my first research questions for my classroom observations:

1. What interactional resources related to power are available to teachers in classrooms?
2. What interactional resources related to power are available to students, individually and as a group, in classrooms?
3. How do teachers and students use these resources in interactions that relate to power relationships?

They also led me to a broad range of sociolinguistic literature related to the use of discourse strategies in communication in general, and specifically in classrooms. For references to this literature, see the Appendix.

Analysis of Ethnographic Data: Looking at Power Relations

The data used in the analysis presented here came from three classrooms: a fifth-grade classroom observed in the spring of 1989; a first-grade classroom observed in the fall of 1989; and another fifth-grade classroom observed throughout the 1992–1993 school year. All the teachers were White; students in each classroom were predominantly White, but included African Americans, Asians, and Latinos. Names of students, teachers, schools, and communities have been changed to protect the identities of participants.

In the first classroom, the teacher was Aileen Corvo, who had been teaching elementary school for over 15 years. There was also a student teacher, Courtney Bridgestone. The class was part of an upper-elementary school that served all the fifth- and sixth-grade students in a small city. In the school, there were students from all socioeconomic levels; Ms. Corvo's classroom, which served the lowest achieving students in the school, included a high proportion of students of low socioeconomic status.

This classroom was highly structured and offered few obvious (but many less obvious) opportunities for students to make choices or construct power relationships. Ms. Corvo believed that tight structures and much teacher control were necessary for effective learning, at least with this group of students, and Ms. Bridgestone usually followed her lead.

The teacher in the second classroom was Sunny Kaminski, who had been teaching for 5 years. Hers was a heterogeneously grouped, whole-language-based first grade in a semirural elementary school. Her classroom, like the school, was economically diverse, including middle-class children whose parents worked in the nearby small city, working-class children whose parents worked in the trades or in local canning and freezing plants, and children who lived in rural poverty. Ms. Kaminski believed that giving students many choices was an important way to encourage them to learn, and her classroom was relatively loosely structured.

The third classroom was a fifth grade in a suburban elementary school; Sue Anderson, the teacher, had over 20 years experience. Students identified as gifted were removed from the heterogeneous group for reading and math instruction, but not for other subjects, so the class was sometimes fully heterogeneous and sometimes, what I like to call lopped heterogeneous, with the "top" students missing. The school served students from two suburbs, one quite wealthy and the other having a mixture of economic levels. A few students were from the adjacent city and attended the school under a court-ordered voluntary integration plan. Most of the children were middle- or upper-middle-class; a few were lower in socioeconomic status. Several students or their parents were born in other countries.

Ms. Anderson believed that students need choices for effective learning. She made substantial efforts to "turn over some of her control" to them, but her classroom continued to have many traditional and structured aspects as well. Of all the classrooms, it was the one in which students and teachers were most fully invested in the colluded-on agenda of cooperation; Ms. Anderson's process of classroom goal setting, focused as it was on the social aspects of classroom life, had created a classroom in which public dissension was minimized.

As I worked on analyzing the data, I became aware of a contradiction. As they talked with me, the teachers claimed their "teacher power" in their classrooms. Yet, there were many instances in the data of teachers contributing to the construction of power relationships in ways that seemed to soften the edges of their claims to control student actions. They disguised their power moves by using indirect discourse strategies (e.g., asking students if they would like to do something when the intention was to tell them to do it), and by using nonverbal cues and classroom arrangements that let their contribution to power relationships remain invisible. Students, too, often used the edges of physical and interactional space for their power-related actions (e.g., moving out of sight of teachers or waiting until their backs were turned), rather than confronting teachers directly.

These observations confirmed that something other than teacher power must be an influential part of the cultural notion of the classroom and added to the strength of McDermott and Tylbor's (1986) ideas about colluded-on agendas. There certainly were times when students forced teachers to reveal what they were doing, as the students asserted their own interpretations of the classroom situation and worked to develop areas of self-determination. Sometimes, too, teachers were quite direct with students. But teachers and students alike seemed to prefer keeping their conflicts in the shadows.

RESEARCH PROCESSES

I began by observing Ms. Corvo's fifth-grade classroom over the course of the spring semester, having gained entree through participation in another research project sponsored by professors in the college of education where I was then studying. Although I had at this point no definite idea of what direction my research process would take me, I took hundreds of pages of field notes on the interactions I observed. I worked like an anthropologist, approaching a new culture and seeking to record events and language for future study and analysis, without having decided in advance what would be significant for that analysis.

I also videotaped, with the help of a colleague, 5 hours of interaction in this classroom, setting up the camera in a rear corner of the room. I interviewed both the teacher and the student teacher to get their impressions of what was taking place, and was able to use my colleague's interviews with the student teacher, in which she often discussed her thoughts about what had happened on the videotape. During the course of the semester I spent in the classroom, I transcribed the notes and indexed the videotapes and the audiotapes of the interviews.

Toward the end of this period of data collection, I located a focus for my research. I wanted to look at what was happening with respect to power in the classroom. "If I were Ms. Bridgestone's supervisor," I said to a colleague, "I would be worried about the way she seems to be seeking more and more power, more and more control, over the children. At first I felt comfortable with what she seemed to be trying to do, but now she seems to be shortening the fence around them every time I go in, so that they have less and less room to do as they please." Further thought and discussion led me to recognize a research topic of considerable interest to me. This was the point at which I used the articles previously discussed—by McDermott and Roth (1978), Wolcott (1987), McDermott and Tylbor (1986), and Mishler (1972)—to begin developing a framework for analysis of these data.

Building on these ideas, I conducted a wide-ranging search of the literature on classroom interaction to learn what other researchers had thought were interactional resources available to students and teachers, and to understand how these resources were used. I believed this process would result in a richer look at the interactions in my data than would have resulted from a search for salient themes in the data itself.

The next fall, I found another classroom in which I would be welcome as a researcher: Sunny Kaminski's first grade. The nature of my data collection had changed because I now had a strong focus for my research. Though I tried to record as much as I could of what I saw in this new environment, I found myself constantly connecting what I was seeing to my developing thoughts about power relations, and that influenced what I noticed and recorded. At the same time, later analysis of the data uncovered many interactions I had not been aware of at the time. In addition to the observation and note taking, I made three hours of videotape of Ms. Kaminski's classroom, and interviewed her both formally and informally, audiotaping the more formal interviews. Together we viewed the videotapes, and I also audiotaped our comments on what we saw. Again, I transcribed my notes and indexed the video- and audiotapes.

At this point, I was ready to bring together the lists of interactional resources that I had found in the literature and the actions I had observed in the two classrooms. The wide variety of ideas with which I began would eventually collapse into four larger categories that form the sixth through ninth chapters of this book: the planned organization of the classroom, discourse choices by teachers, the ways that the question of what will count as classroom knowledge was decided, and the ways that students opposed teachers' agendas.

Three years later, I was able to spend an hour or more a week during the whole school year taking notes in Sue Anderson's classroom. I was unable to videotape, and most of my interactions with Ms. Anderson were informal interviews, on which I took notes. Again, I transcribed the notes I had made. This body of data I used differently—as a richer source from which to draw examples of the kinds of interactions I had already defined as relevant. Also, it served to confirm for me the validity of the ideas I had developed. In this fifth grade so different in style from Ms. Corvo's fifth-grade classroom, I could see power relationships being constructed in much the same way as in the other two classrooms.

In order to understand as well as possible the words and actions of students and teachers within the classroom, I needed to look at them very closely and with sophisticated lenses. I used methods and concepts from ethnomethodology, sociolinguistics, discourse analysis, and microethnography to see how teachers and students contribute to the development of the power relationships within which they live. (Some items from the literature of each of these traditions are listed in the Appendix.) I tried to see the meaning of familiar classroom events in terms of a developing notion of power relationships.

In this analysis, I sought to combine qualities of both rigor and openness. Rigor was represented by an emphasis on triangulation of data and the preservation of negative evidence in the analysis. It also appeared, I believe, in the use of extensive description and narrative, or story—an effective means of promoting understanding of human actions. Gregory Bateson (1979) remarked that, "A story is a little knot or complex of that species of connectedness which we call relevance" (p. 14). When actions are considered in context, story results. It seems to organize information so that it can be located and processed, enhance the abilities of memory

(Spence, 1984), and allow the expression of insights that cannot be stated directly by the teller.

This storytelling is related to the "thick description" of ethnography (Geertz, 1973). The *thick description* is, in effect, the story; analysis may usefully point out aspects of the story for consideration, but all the content is in the story. Because the hermeneutic point of view (Gadamer, 1976) assumes the need for rich context for understanding, any research undertaken from this point of view will require the provision of thick description unless the thing to be studied, like a literary text, can actually be shared with the reader.

Story is also a crucial tool for the reader in evaluating the credibility of research. Without an understanding of the context of the data, readers cannot be expected to determine whether the reality experienced by the researcher is related to their own realities. Thus, story is important in both the doing and the using of research.

* * *

Within the highly defined space called a classroom, the interactive conception of power that I am using gives far greater weight to the actions of students than does the traditional definition. It makes it impossible to impose on teachers the total responsibility for classroom environments and outcomes that has traditionally been theirs, and at the same time requires close examination of student contributions to those environments and outcomes. In the long run, it demands careful inquiry not only about cultures and social structures that teachers bring to classrooms, but also about those brought by students.

PART I

NARRATIVES OF CLASSROOM LIFE

৪৩ ◆ ৫৪

Chapter 2

Sunny Kaminski's First-Grade Classroom: A Typical Readers' Workshop Time

� ◆ ෮

Sunny Kaminski sits in her rocking chair, reading a story to 22 eager listeners. The first graders sit cross-legged on the rug, enjoying both the story and the fall sunshine that pours through the window above them. When she finishes the story, Ms. Kaminski says, "Tell you what. If you would come over here and choose a book and then find someplace in the room to read it, it would be just great." Children scatter to find a favorite book or a new and challenging one, and to sit at tables or desks, on the rug or on the lap of the class bear. Everyone begins to read. This is reading-workshop time in Sunny Kaminski's first grade.

THE COMMUNITY

Ms. Kaminski's room is one of two first grades at Roseton Elementary School in a rural county in a southeastern state. The county, surrounding the university city of Charter Hills, includes both nearby suburban areas and rural and agricultural areas stretching about 15 miles in each direction from the city. It includes residential subdivisions, large farms and plantations belonging to wealthy owners, small but prosperous farms, and undeveloped areas where natural beauty and rural poverty are intertwined.

Roseton School is 12 miles east of Charter Hills and only a mile or two from the mountains. Its economic diversity is considerable. Some of its students come from middle-class or working-class homes; their parents may work away from town or commute to Charter Hills. Others live in rural poverty, in houses that look as though a strong wind could knock them down or in mobile homes, beside the highway or at the end of a dirt road in the woods. A few African-American and Latino families have children attending Roseton, but most students are White.

THE SCHOOL

Roseton Elementary School is a one-story building with two wings and a central core containing offices, a cafeteria, and a gym and multipurpose room. Classrooms for Grades 3 through 5 are in one wing; kindergarten and first-, and second-grade classes are in the other. Ceramic-tiled halls are brightened by children's art and writing. The front hallway serves as a display area for big projects from various classes; tables might hold dioramas of local plants and animals or colorful sculptures created by children.

During the 3 years before I began my research, Roseton moved away from the use of basal readers and other textbooks toward a whole-language approach to reading and writing and toward more manipulatives and more problem solving in mathematics. This change has been greatest in the primary grades, and as you walk down their hallway, you can see classrooms with open carpeted areas and round tables, children moving freely from room to room, and children reading, writing, or painting in the hallway itself.

Roseton School has a family feel. A few students come and go each year, but many remain in the district for a long time. Teachers are aware of the families their students come from, and frequently find brothers and sisters and cousins in their classes in successive years. They have long-term relationships with adult family members, getting to know them through the parent conferences that, together with written narratives, replace report cards in the primary grades. Classroom volunteers are welcome; they include mothers, some with toddlers in tow, and "foster grandparents" from local retirement communities.

THE CLASS

Ms. Kaminski's class was one of two heterogeneously grouped first grades. Some children, moving up from kindergarten, were expected to present special challenges to their teachers; principal and teachers worked together to distribute them fairly evenly between the classes and to match each one with the teacher who might better meet his or her needs. Thus, Ms. Kaminski's class of 22 included 2 children reading fluently when school began, and 4 or 5 children quite unsure of alphabet letters and sounds, with little or no sense of themselves as readers. Of 2 children who had been retained in first grade from the previous year, 1 was in this classroom; he was among the nonreaders.

The class included 9 girls and 13 boys; this was a year when there were fewer than usual first graders to divide between the two classrooms. Five children were African American, 16 were White, and 1 was Latina. One child, the boy who had been retained, was labeled *learning disabled*; 5 others—2 African-American boys, 2 African American girls, and the Latina girl—were classified as *at-risk* on the basis of teacher recommendations and assessments. This meant that a reading teacher was supposed to take each of them out of the room for a brief, daily period of one-on-one instruction. One boy, not counted as a member of the class, was assigned to the resource room on a full-time basis. He was occasionally in the classroom; during the observations he lined up with the children for physical education and participated in the play they put on.

Adults in the Classroom

Sunny Kaminski was in her fifth year of teaching, all at Roseton Elementary. She had taught kindergarten, transitional first grade, and first grade. Her head of blond curls, energetic body, and ready smile seemed to match her enthusiastic and optimistic style.

Ms. Kaminski attended high school in a nearby county after having lived with her family in various parts of the United States, and graduated from the school of education at a state university near her home. She was hired to teach at Roseton shortly after she graduated. She enthusiastically supports the school's move from basal readers toward a whole language approach. She took graduate courses in education at the university in Charter Hills and understands herself to be a thoughtful and reflective teacher.

Ms. Kaminski's complex concerns about the lives and learning of "her" children are reflected in everything she says about them. There is no aspect of classroom life she has not thought about and tried to regulate to promote the children's growth and learning. She has a seemingly limitless fund of knowledge about each child, and expects to consider the changing circumstances of their outside-of-school lives in her planning. For example, while one child's parents were separated, she repeatedly mentioned that fact in understanding his daily behavior and in finding ways to support him.

Ms. Kaminski is also acutely aware of each child's progress in learning to read and write and in other areas. Each interaction with the children is an opportunity to gather information about their status as learners; she constantly considers this body of information as she plans activities for readers' and writers' workshop times, or suggests specific books or groups of books that certain children might read. Even the amount and tone of the encouragement or challenge she provides for each child is based on this information.

Ms. Kaminski believes that children learn best when they have many choices in the learning process, and she expects children to respond positively when they realize that her classroom is "a pretty good place for them to be." Her planning for the classroom is based on these two ideas. This means that she plans many choices for the children, not that they can do anything they like. She lets them know what she expects in terms of behavior and learning activities, and she believes they will see these expectations as reasonable.

Ms. Kaminski's is an active classroom. Children move around freely during most parts of the day. They work alone, in self-created groups, or, occasionally, in assigned groups. Sometimes they are assisted by various adults. Most of the time, they are free to talk and interact with whomever they wish, and the classroom is usually buzzing with student voices. Patterns of movement and of expectations in the classroom are parallel; times when children are moving throughout the room and have many choices are succeeded by gathering-in times, when children are physically grouped on the rug and have fewer choices.

There are rules in the classroom, though, and establishing these rules was the focus of the first few days of school. Children are expected to choose from among the alternatives designated as acceptable during each part of the day. They are expected to respect the property and persons of other students. Hitting is a serious offense in this classroom, and the principal is ready to support Ms. Kaminski in case anyone breaks this rule.

One day, I saw Ms. Kaminski notice two boys hitting one another. The incident did not seem particularly serious—no one was very upset by it—but Ms. Kaminski called them to her and immediately sent them to the office to tell the principal what they had done. They were not to return to the classroom until they had talked to the principal and stayed with her for a while to think about their offense. Ms. Kaminski said this kind of prompt response to any hitting was what made it a rare event in her classroom.

Ms. Kaminski sometimes scolded children who were not meeting her expectations, but more often she either stated those expectations and their consequences or used some "creative" way of gaining cooperation. "You've got a ma-a-ah-velous line, dahlings," she said to a group of slightly wiggly children, who suddenly did have a marvelous (straight and quiet) line.

Sunny Kaminski was rarely alone with her students in the classroom. Two other adults were there regularly—a student teacher and an aide. Among the three women active in the room, Ms. Kaminski's position could be distinguished by the fact that children almost always approached her, rather than the others, with problems and concerns of all kinds. She was constantly interrupted in what she was doing; the other two almost never were. Thus, the actions of the children marked her as "the teacher."

There were also other adults in the classroom at various times. The reading and "at-risk" teacher often worked in the room with the whole group or with the five children assigned to her, though at other times she would remove one of those children from the room. Two parent volunteers and a "foster grandparent" came regularly to read or work with the children.

The Classroom's Appearance

Ms. Kaminski's classroom was full of interesting objects. It was not exactly crowded; a large space was opened up for group gatherings, and in most parts of the classroom there was plenty of room to move freely. But everywhere there was something to look at.

The room is a large one and very light, with a big window on the wall opposite the door. The walls are painted white or tan, and most of the floor is carpeted. The room was divided roughly into thirds: The third nearest the window was left open for group gatherings, divided by a book display rack between the open area and the library area; the middle third contained three large round tables, the easel, and the water table; and the third nearest the door was divided by cubbies and shelves to form a block play area, a house corner, and an art area with a long table. When the 22 children were spread out around the room, it did not seem at all crowded, though it could certainly seem busy and noisy.

In the library area, Ms. Kaminski displayed dozens of trade books. A nearly life-sized stuffed bear, won at an amusement park, sat in the corner, ready to shelter one or two readers. Math materials were on low shelves next to the gathering rug. The cages of hamsters and guinea pigs were also in this part of the room. Ms. Kaminski had a rocking chair to sit in, and there was a stereo and a box of rhythm instruments near it.

The three round tables were always being moved to slightly different spots to suit the needs of the moment; next to one of them was the class computer, which was often in use for reading and math activities and games. The block area was supplied with blocks and accessories, and the house corner had a variety of materials for "pretending." Many different papers and art materials were available for the children, and the three-sided painting easel got heavy use.

If Ms. Kaminski's room was cluttered, its size kept the clutter from being oppressive. Most of the items placed on tables and on top of shelves were for children to look at and use; there were closets near the door for storage.

By November, the walls were almost covered with children's work and with various posters. A tour of the room suggests this abundance: By the hall door was the door to the bathroom; it was covered with "environmental print": words cut from boxes and wrappers, brought in by the children. In the tiny bathroom were posters of the text of two "big books," one in front of and one behind the toilet. Next was a bulletin board labeled "Parents' Corner," a small area with pamphlets and notices of interest to parents. Then a display of students' work, then a bulletin board showing everyone's birthday, a display of student paintings, and an ABC chart. Turning the corner to the window wall, there was more student work, and an "Our Favorite Authors" bulletin board almost covered by a large mural the children had made. Wax paper leaves and cutouts of bats were taped to the window, and a counting chart and job chart filled up the window wall. In the corner was a large easel used for charts and big books, and next to the chalkboard, a calendar. On the chalkboard were lists of "Words the Class Knows," a poster about leaves, and student work. Behind the computer was a sign-up area where children reserved a turn on the computer, and then more posters from language experience lessons. The American flag hung at the end of the chalkboard next to a poster about the Pledge of Allegiance, and more language experience posters turned the corner and filled up the space to the door. These walls were always changing, like mirrors reflecting the curriculum as it developed.

The Daily Schedule

About 8:00 a.m., children started to arrive on buses or be dropped off by their parents. The day would ease in as some went to breakfast, others turned in "homework assignments" (e.g., "Write something with an orange crayon or marker in honor of the university football game tomorrow"), or did them if they weren't done the night before. Gradually more children would arrive and the pace would pick up; this was called Free Choice Time, and children were allowed to select any of a variety of available activities in the room, including reading, writing, using art materials, painting, water play, blocks, playing house, holding a guinea pig, and so forth.

Everyone was expected to use the math materials at some time during this period, so the round tables often held children making patterns, counting blocks, or balancing number scales. There were always one or two children, usually boys, playing math games on the computer. After the winter break, the children were given math workbooks, and often worked in those at this time.

Cleanup time was at 9:15, and by 9:25, everyone was gathered on the rug for the first sharing time of the day. This might be a time for children to show their homework (once the assignment was to make something about Native Americans, and everything from a home-lashed lance to a model village made from paper cups came in), to share stories or events in their lives (once Carlton showed his fingernail that was falling off because he slammed it with a rock), or to read a book brought from home. They usually began with a song, sung along with a tape, and sometimes accompanied by rhythm instruments.

About 9:45, readers' workshop began. There was no definite pattern from day to day. Sometimes, everyone was asked to choose a book and read, with a reminder that they would be sharing their books at the end. At these times, adults circulated to read with various children. Sometimes selected children were placed in groups with Ms. Kaminski, the aide, or other adults. On other days, each adult had a list of children to read with in the course of the morning. At still other times, there was a planned activity, for which the children were usually divided into groups. In such groups, they might read and illustrate a poem given to them on a handout or they might be introduced to a new group of books that Ms. Kaminski thought were suited to their needs.

Readers' workshop usually continued until 10:30, which was snacktime. Most often, children finished what they were doing when 10:30 came, ate their snacks, and then gathered on the rug for sharing time. This might include children reading aloud from books they had used that morning, children putting on a "readers' theater," in which two or three children read a book aloud together, or Ms. Kaminski reading aloud. At 11:00, the physical education teacher came to get the children for half an hour in the gym or outdoors.

When they returned, it was time for writers' workshop. They might begin with a minilesson about a topic like the usefulness of separating words as you write to make it easier to read them later, or a specific sound and how it is written. Children were expected to use invented spellings in their writing, but also to be able to profit from information that would let them refine those spellings. Writers might draw pictures and write about them, work on "books" or stories that they had started on previous days, or write in journals kept in notebooks and composition books. Children were often working in groups or pairs, and adults were circulating to help and encourage. Writers' workshop usually included a sharing time, when children could read their writings to the class and get responses from the others.

Lunch was at 12:30, followed by an outdoor recess and a time for special activities in science, social studies, and literature. These were often organized as units that would last for a week or more. The school day ended at 2:30.

Most of the observations for this study took place during readers' workshop, from about 9:45 to 11:00 each morning, and included the snack time. This description of a typical readers' workshop comprises incidents that really happened, though not necessarily on the same day. Words of teachers and children, as well as incidents, come from field notes and videotapes. To give the reader a context for understanding the analysis chapters, some incidents will reappear in those chapters.

A TYPICAL READERS' WORKSHOP

Free choice time and cleanup are over, and most of the children are gathered on the rug ready to start their sharing time. Ms. Kaminski is sitting in her rocking chair, and she speaks to several of the children.

"Thomas, sit front and center." "Carlton, sit on your bottom." "Andra, sit up please." "See how Juana, Jimmy, and Steve are sitting close to the front so they can see the pictures."

Erin has written a story she wants to read to the class. She stands up in front of them, ready to start.

Ms. Kaminski says to Erin, "I hear a lot of voices. Do you think the children are ready to listen, or ready to sing?"

Erin says, "Sing," and sits back down. They do sing two songs with a tape playing on the stereo. Ms. Kaminski flips a chart to the page where the words of the song are written and hands a pointer to Mandy, who points to the words as they go along. (Learning to point to words as they are read is considered an important reading skill here.) Mandy is pretty successful at this, but sometimes moves too slowly, and Ms. Kaminski takes her wrist and helps her move the pointer.

Two boys go over to the stereo, pick up rhythm instruments from the box under it, and start to play. Three other boys not yet sitting on the rug are watching a caterpillar in a terrarium.

At the end of the song, Ms. Kaminski praises the playing of the musicians.

A girl says, "They're not musicians."

Ms. Kaminski answers, "Musicians are people who make music. Weren't they making music with the bells and the tambourine? Then they're musicians!"

Erin stands up and reads her book to the children, who are quite attentive. Now Ms. Kaminski calls the boys who are looking at the caterpillar to come to the rug. She sends Erin, whose book was about caterpillars, to put it on the science book shelf. Noah has been taking off and playing with his bolo tie; she sends him to his cubby to put it away.

"I asked you twice to put it on and keep it on," she says. The net result of all this is that there are constantly one or two children off the rug.

Now, Ms. Kaminski holds up a book by Eric Carle, tells the students that he is the author (an important word in this class because the students are encouraged to see themselves as authors), and asks what other books Eric Carle wrote. (She expects that someone can answer this because his *The Very Hungry Caterpillar* (1989) is one of the most popular books with these children.)

Carlton says, "Elephants."

Ms. Kaminski answers, "Yes, this is an elephant on the front of the book. What else did he write?"

Carlton holds up a book he has written. "I wanta share this."

Ms. Kaminski says firmly, "Not now, Carlton. We can share later." Nick raises his hand.

Ms. Kaminski nods at him and he says, "The Very Hungry Caterpillar."

"Right," she replies, and opens the book and starts to read it. She stops frequently to let the children predict what will be on the next page or to hear their comments on the book. Most children are watching and listening attentively. Philip is lying half across one of the tables, and two other boys have moved to chairs on the edges of the rug. Jessica scoots over to the aide; she sucks her thumb while she leans on the aide's knees. When Ms. Kaminski is finished, she picks up a portable book rack that contains a set of very easy reading books. She reminds the children that they have these books and displays their titles and pictures.

"These are good books for most of you to choose during readers' workshop," she says. Then she tells them that now they will have readers' workshop and that today they can go and choose the books they want to read. And she wants everyone to be working.

She continues, "If you don't make great choices today or if you don't work real well we're going to have little groups to talk about making choices." (This could be a kind of threat, but it is early in the year, and it sounds more as though she is saying it to justify to herself her plan for letting them make free choices and for responding if this does not work out well.)

Philip raises his hand and describes what he plans to do during readers' workshop.

Ms. Kaminski responds, "Oh, great, that's a terrific choice to make in readers' workshop." She adds a warning, "I don't want to see anyone running around the room and playing. You should be doing your job."

"Now, go for it!" she continues, and the children get up and move over to the bookshelves and the library corner.

Within a few minutes, most of the children have settled with books at tables, on the rug in the library corner, and at the table in the house corner. Ms. Kaminski, the aide, and the student teacher are all at the tables, talking with and assisting informal groups of children. Jessica is sitting on the student teacher's lap, sucking her thumb, while the student teacher points to the words in a book she is reading aloud. Nick is reading the big book on the easel.

Jimmy has the raccoon puppet and is squeaking it noisily on the rug. Charles and Noah are wrestling in the library corner, hidden from the view of any of the adults. Jimmy's play with the raccoon puppet starts to get rougher. Buster comes in the door (he has been with the learning disabilities teacher) and sits down to look at the caterpillars. When Ms. Kaminski finishes what she is doing at one of the tables, she goes over to the rug and talks quietly to Jimmy. He goes to the bookshelf, picks up a magazine, and sits down to read it, still holding the puppet.

Next, Ms. Kaminski goes over to the corner where another boy has joined the group of wrestlers. She puts out her hand to Charles, and he gets up and walks with her to the bookshelves, where they pick out a book and then sit down on the rug to read together. This seems to end the wrestling, and the other two boys choose books and lean on the giant stuffed bear. Suddenly, the room is much quieter and more peaceful.

The reading teacher comes in to read with Jimmy. Buster moves over to join a group with the aide. On the rug, Philip and Mandy start to argue about which of them will have a certain book.

Ms. Kaminski notices this and looks up. "Ma-a-an-dee," she says. They separate, Mandy taking the book. She sits down to read. Pearl goes over to the bookshelf and gets a nursery rhyme book. She sits down on the rug with it and is making animal noises to go with the pictures.

Philip is walking around on the rug; he is the only one in the room who is not involved with a book. Carlton has been sitting on the rug, reading a book to a puppet. He notices Philip, gets up, and starts to pat and poke Philip with the puppet, but Philip ignores him. Ms. Kaminski picks up one of the easy books, which she showed the children earlier. She takes Carlton, who is still holding the puppet, on her lap in a chair. Together they read the book.

Pearl approaches Ms. Kaminski. "Is it time for snack?"

Loud enough to be heard by all the children, Ms. Kaminski answers, "OK, you can get out your snacks at 10:30 when the long hand gets to the 6. Keep an eye on the clock if you like but we'll let you know when it's time."

Philip is talking noisily with Mandy on the rug, apparently arguing about who is going to read a book and who is going to listen. It appears that they are less interested in who will have the book than in being noisy and silly. Philip sits down and says he will read the book aloud to Mandy, but he only flips through the pages. Then he goes to the big book on the easel, picks up the pointer, and starts to read aloud and point to the words.

Jimmy gets two *Ranger Rick* magazines and sits down at a table to read them. Only about 14 of the 22 children are involved with books now, but this is not surprising because the allotted time for reader's workshop is now over.

Pearl stands in front of the clock, and says loudly, "The long hand is on the 6."

A chorus of "Snack! Snack! It's time for snack!" rises around the room. Most of the children quickly put away their books and get their lunch boxes. Carrie and Susan take the big bucket that holds the snack and milk money and leave for the cafeteria. Two or three children who are buying lunch don't have a snack. The aide gets a bag of raisins and gives each one a handful on a napkin.

Within 5 minutes, some children are finished eating and have gotten books or are playing on the rug. Buster is in the rocking chair and is scooting it around the rug. Ms. Kaminski suggests to Nat that he look at the caterpillars, and he does.

Now, most of the children are finished eating, and Ms. Kaminski says, "OK, I want all the boys and girls on the rug." They gather there fairly quickly, but are not quiet yet. Ms. Kaminski asks children to put away some of the things they are holding. The noise level goes way down.

"Carlton, this is your one warning," says Ms. Kaminski. (The rule is that if someone gets a warning and does not comply he or she will have to sit at a table away from the group.) "Go put that on the bookshelf, please. Sit here with nothing in your hands." Carlton puts away the book and sits down.

Ms. Kaminski opens the big book of nursery rhymes that is on the easel and starts the tape. She uses a stick to point to the words as the reader on the tape proceeds. Most of the children are sitting quietly, looking and listening. Nat has on a pair of earphones that are not connected to the tape player. Another rhyme comes on the tape. The room is so quiet that sounds from other rooms and from the hall are heard for the first time. "Hickory, dickory, dock" comes on the tape, and the children start to read aloud with it. The reader on the tape pauses, and Andra goes right on. Ms. Kaminski hears this and realizes that Andra knows the rhyme by heart. She stops the tape and takes Andra up on her lap to say the verse aloud to the class.

The aide is sitting on a chair near where Nat and Noah have on earphones. She leans over to Nat and asks him to take them off. He raises his eyebrows and looks like he has never heard of such a thing as taking them off, but he complies.

Ms. Kaminski tells the group that they will see what is going on in the insect cage before they go to gym. They get up and gather around it. Most of them are looking at the new chrysalis that she shows them, but two boys are playing with some markers. She picks up a small cage and holds it up to show them that the cricket is eating the ants. Now all the children except Buster are looking at one or the other of the cages.

Ms. Kaminski asks Carlton to go across the hall and tell the other first-grade teacher that they have a new chrysalis.

"How would you say that?" she asks.

"Do y'all wanta see the chrysalis?" Carlton replies. She nods and he leaves on his errand.

"Tell you what," says Ms. Kaminski. "If you are ready you can get in line for gym." Most of the children line up by the door.

To the rest she says, "OK, if the rest of you want to take a look at the insects, then when Mr. Johnson comes you'll get in line."

Ms. Kaminski goes to the door, and starts to teach finger spelling to those in line. Many are practicing with her. The front of the line is very quiet, but those in the back are wiggling and turning around. Ms. Kaminski reminds them of the rules for the hall, that they should walk and whisper. The physical education teacher appears.

"Let's go," says the student teacher.

"Just a minute," says Thad, who is writing with chalk on the painting easel. He finishes and follows the line out the door.

* * *

This is a typical reader's workshop time in Sunny Kaminski's room because it exemplifies both the structure and the tone that were regularities of the classroom. In terms of structure, the interplay of choice and expectation that emerges from this account of Sunny Kaminski's classroom is one of its most outstanding features. Children have many choices, but each choice is within the framework of expectations that Ms. Kaminski has constructed. And it is her belief *that making choices will help children learn*. Thus, each time children make choices—whether it is a choice of where to be, of what to read, of whom to work with, of whom to ask for help—they are meeting Ms. Kaminski's expectations.

Also, the regular sequence of activities—the time for gathering on the rug, the time in which children are freely moving about and making choices, the snack, and the second gathering on the rug before leaving—is repeated day after day. Within it can be found many variations. Different activities take place during the gatherings on the rug, depending on what Ms. Kaminski wants to share with the children each day, on what their home-work has been or what they have done during the rest of the reader's workshop, or on what the children suggest. It is not unusual for some or all of the children to participate in planned group activities, with or without adults. Any of the three main activities can be shortened or lengthened at will. But children can expect that the sequence will be the same almost every day.

The tone, too, is typical of Ms. Kaminski's room. Ms. Kaminski speaks courteously to the children, but expresses her expectations for their actions quite clearly. Children feel free to ask questions, to choose activities, and to engage in some play that is clearly outside the limits of Ms. Kaminski's expressed expectations. She often chooses to change children's behavior, not through scolding or punishment, but by introducing a more appropriate activity. And most of the time, children are as pleasant to Ms. Kaminski and to other children as she is to them.

Chapter 3

Aileen Corvo's Fifth-Grade Classroom: A Typical Language Arts Period

80 ◆ 03

Ms. Corvo stands at the front of her crowded classroom, ready to begin.

"Give me your attention," she says. "That's right, your undivided attention—only on me, the Golden Girl."

Aside to Ms. Bridgestone, a student teacher, she adds, "I love that show!"

"I need your attention and I'm not waiting much longer," she tells the class. This is the beginning of a language arts period in Ms. Corvo's fifth-grade classroom.

THE COMMUNITY

Aileen Corvo's classroom was one of several fifth grades at Grove Upper Elementary School in Charter Hills. The town of about 50,000 is home to a good-sized university in a southeastern state. Its African-American and White residents live in both attractive residential areas, expensive and not-so-expensive, and areas of deteriorated homes and public housing. Most land within the city has already been developed for residential or commercial purposes, which has spread into the surrounding county. Although not one of its state's largest cities, Charter Hills functions as an urban center.

THE SCHOOL

Until the year in which I observed Aileen Corvo's classroom, Charter Hills students in kindergarten through Grade 5 had attended neighborhood elementary schools. Students in Grades 6 through 8 had attended one of two middle schools located on opposite sides of the city. Grove was widely perceived as "better" than the other middle school—in part because it had fewer students of color—and concerns for equity had led to a reorganization. Starting with this school year, the neighborhood elementary schools served only students in Grades kindergarten through 4; all fifth- and sixth-grade students attended one of the former middle schools, renamed Grove Upper Elementary School; and all seventh- and eighth-grade students attended the other.

This made the 1988–1989 school year one of change for everyone at Grove. All the students in the school were new to it, as both the fifth- and sixth-graders had attended neighborhood elementary schools the previous year. Over half the teachers had either moved to Grove from a neighborhood school or the other middle school, or were newly hired. Also, student enrollment had increased with the change; there were now nearly 600 students and every room was full. The strong community that principals and teachers had developed over several years together had been stretched beyond its limits; the work of creating it had to be started again.

Teachers at the school said that a high priority had been placed on ensuring that students from all the neighborhood schools were represented in every classroom. This policy was intended to promote the racial integra-tion that was a major goal of the reorganization. Previously, the school had practiced at least semiheterogeneous grouping; now students were grouped by achievement, with the highest achieving students from all the schools grouped together, and so on. Ms. Corvo's classroom received a group of low-achieving students from all parts of the district.

Teachers and administrators had considerable concern about maintain-ing discipline in the school, at least in part because it was now receiving more children from neighborhoods thought likely to produce trouble-makers. Most of school's administrators had remained, and they made little concession to differences between a middle school (Grades 6–8) and an upper elementary school (Grades 5–6). Although students in the school were much younger than before, systems of detention and suspension that had been in place in the middle school were retained and strengthened. For example, a fifth-grade girl from Ms. Corvo's room who punched another student was suspended from school for 5 days, probably a harsher punish-ment than she would have received in elementary school.

Also, the organization of the school was not changed to meet the needs of younger children. Classes were still departmentalized; students still moved as a group from room to room through the entire day; teachers were still assigned to work in teams of subject matter specialists. Because team members were new to one another, and had little time to develop relation-ships and practices to make teaming successful, during this school year, teacher morale at Grove was quite low.

Physically, the school comprises three buildings: a gym with health classrooms; a fine and applied arts building with an auditorium and rooms for band, orchestra, art, and home economics; and a two-story building set on a hill, with the office, locker areas, and cafeteria on the lower floor and classrooms set in a square around the media center on the main floor. The school is quite modern in appearance, built of dark-brown brick; the main floor, carpeted throughout, is climate controlled, with few windows.

THE CLASS

There were 20 children in Ms. Corvo's class, 13 boys and 7 girls. Twelve children were White, 7 African-American, and 1 Asian. Socioeconomic levels were varied, including a few children from middle-class homes, and more from working-class and poor homes. Two White middle-class boys were labeled learning disabled and were receiving resource help. Another boy was in the process of being assessed because his teachers believed he had a learning disability. Two children were receiving services from the school psychologist because of severe problems at home. A few of the students were reading on grade level; most were not.

The Teachers

Aileen Corvo is an experienced teacher, nominated in the past for the "Teacher of the Year" award in her district. A short woman with a rounded figure and curly black hair, she presents herself in a dramatic manner. Words seem to pour out of her. I found it almost impossible to make verbatim notes of her talk. When she gave directions, they were a flood of commands, suggestions, explanations, and comments. Her speech was not particularly loud, but very intense, with much variety in its intonation. She used many strong gestures, her arms and hands moving far out from her body as she spoke.

I observed her class through the spring, during the last months of a year she had found very difficult. She had been teaching for several years in one of the more affluent elementary school districts in the city, and in that school she had always worked with classes that were grouped quite heterogeneously. In the early part of this school year, she told Grove's principal how unhappy she was with the homogeneous grouping of students that had resulted in her low-achieving class, but her protests were ignored. What she said about the behavior and learning of the class, and about her own feelings, implied that by spring she was trying to get through the rest of the year in a difficult situation, in the hope that next year would be better. When I visited her classroom after Memorial Day to take some photographs, she told me she had wanted to apply for a transfer, but had been too tired to start the process.

Ms. Corvo was a "clinical instructor," or supervising teacher, in the teacher education program at the local university. At the end of February she began to supervise the teaching internship of Courtney Bridgestone, a longtime resident of Charter Hills who had attended Grove School herself when it was a junior high school. She graduated from the local university and worked elsewhere in the state for a few years before enrolling in a teacher certification and master's degree program in elementary education.

Ms. Bridgestone is a tall, slim young woman with ash blond hair; she dresses in simple yet elegant-looking clothes, often wearing gray, black, and white. Her physical appearance seems in keeping with her manner, which is usually subdued and calm. She spoke to the class in quiet and businesslike tones, telling them what they needed to know and what she wanted them to do in a minimum of words. This style contrasted sharply with Ms. Corvo's more voluble and dramatic self-presentation. Ms. Bridgestone's gestures, too, were very controlled; she kept her hands close to her body and made small movements. She has a sharp sense of humor, and frequently used it to make a point gently or to defuse a potentially difficult situation.

Ms. Bridgestone said in an interview that she had enjoyed school herself, especially Grove Junior High School, when she had been a student 15 years earlier. She was apprehensive about her internship; she knew that "this particular group of kids were ones that had been quote failures for several years," and worried that it would be hard to interest them in learning.

Also, the discipline system at the school, which was very structured and based on a "thick handbook," conflicted with ideas she had been exposed to about using "a more cooperative approach, giving kids responsibility." She described herself as struggling with determining the best approach in situations of conflict, unsure of her own "philosophy on discipline." Yet, with the students, she nearly always seemed calm and self-assured.

She was afraid, though, that she would get into a situation in which a "student said, 'No, I won't do it,' and, in front of the class, or something like that." She said she had been intimidated by "kids like that" when she was at Grove; she feared they would intimidate her again. What I observed, though, was that the students were less inclined to resist Ms. Bridgestone's more indirectly expressed commands than Ms. Corvo's very directly expressed wishes.

Ms. Corvo talked with me about her class before I visited it. What she said led me to expect to see overt forms of student misbehavior. However, I observed that most of the children were cooperating fairly well most of the time. Later (see chap. 8), I understood how regularly students in this classroom were engaging in relatively subtle forms of resistance to teacher agendas. Yet, only twice did I see a student refuse to comply with a teacher's instructions, and both these confrontations were brief and mild. Most of the children seemed to enjoy the novels they were reading; a few regularly seemed tuned out, but not actively resistant.

During some of the writing workshops, when students were supposed to be working independently on their own projects, there was some off-task activity, and from time to time, Ms. Corvo and Ms. Bridgestone would reprimand the students as a group. Yet, on other days, everyone seemed to be working most of the time, and many of the students appeared to be pleased and proud of their work.

Based on comments the teachers made to me, I speculated that Ms. Corvo's negative view of the students in her class, and Ms. Bridgestone's fear of them, were based on comparisons with other classes and other students. For example, in an interview, Ms. Corvo said that with a different class she would have had multiple reading groups and many projects during the language arts period.

The Classroom's Appearance

Ms. Corvo's classroom was both crowded and cluttered. It had been a science room when Grove School was a middle school, and about one-third of the space was occupied by three permanently fixed lab tables with sinks. Ms. Corvo said that she had "fought to keep those lab tables" because she taught science in the afternoon. She felt this had been her worst mistake because the tables were designed for older children and were too high for many of her students to use. She found a way to use the space between the tables, sending students to work there during writing workshop and placing desks between the lab tables for students she found had the most difficulty staying out of trouble.

Students had individual desks with separate molded plastic chairs. Most of the desks were crowded together in the main part of the room. They were arranged in pairs on either side of a narrow center aisle, facing the chalk-board. Immediately in front of the chalkboard was a narrow space in which Ms. Corvo and Ms. Bridgestone usually stood during large-group instruction. At the back of the room was Ms. Corvo's desk. The registers for the ventilation system were also at the back of the room, and the fans' steady whir was an unchanging accompaniment to classroom activity.

The clutter was increased by jackets hanging on the backs of chairs, and backpacks and band instruments on the floor next to or under desks. There was no closet space available. Students had lockers that they were allowed to visit at certain times of the day, but many did not keep their coats in them, partly because they had to go outdoors to reach the gym and fine arts buildings. The students who had language arts with Ms. Corvo were her homeroom group, and the desks they sat at were "their own." Even though other students used the desks during part of the day, Ms. Corvo's students could keep papers and books in the slot under the writing surface.

The room gave the impression of being quite dark, though I was assured it met state requirements for light levels; the wall opposite the door and part of the back wall were made of the same dark-colored bricks that formed the exterior of the building, and the front wall was painted a medium shade of gray around the chalkboard. Only the wall next to the door was light-colored, and its lower half was lined with dark-colored wood cabinets, originally intended for storage of science materials. The floor was covered with a gray industrial-type carpet. The room's single narrow window was behind Ms. Corvo's desk on the back wall.

The walls held many charts, posters, and bulletin boards of student work, arranged rather haphazardly. One of the posters reminded students to "Maintain Eye Contact," to "Think Positive—Don't Trade Negative Responses," to "Mind Your Own Business," to "Wait Your Turn," and to use words like "Thank You, Excuse Me, May I, Please." Another poster asked students to "Respect Others Through Word and Deed" by speaking in a friendly manner; being honest, fair, and truthful; being slow to anger; and wishing others well. Students were also reminded to "Do Your Job" (complete assignments, follow directions, and have materials) and to "Allow Others to Do Their Job" (work and study quietly, avoid interrupting, and remain silent in the halls). Also posted were reminders about handwriting, how to carry out the writing process, and how to study. It seemed that the walls were visually overwhelming students with directions and orders much as Ms. Corvo did verbally.

Sitting on the lab tables were science materials and piles of books that were used during the afternoon. The tops of file cabinets, storage cabinets, and shelves were piled high with books and papers. Storage boxes sat on the floor in the back corners of the room, and on various surfaces. Ms. Corvo said she missed her "good closets and shelves" from her elementary school classroom.

The Language Arts Period

The language arts period was 95 minutes long (8:15 to 9:50 a.m.), sometimes a little longer if the first activity started during the time designated for homeroom. It was usually divided into three parts. First, on at least 4 days each week, was the spelling or vocabulary lesson. Next, the class nearly always read aloud and discussed the novel (paperback trade book) they were reading, working as a whole group. Occasionally they would form pairs and read to one another. Ms. Corvo said she had begun the year with two separate reading groups, but found that with this class the whole-group instruction was more successful.

Sometimes the students had a worksheet or brief written assignment, related to the novel they were reading, to work on independently while the teachers circulated to help them. This might be a homework assignment to begin during class and finish at home.

The final part of the language arts period was a writers' workshop, which usually began with a brief lesson for the whole group and continued with students writing independently or *conferencing* with a friend on their pieces of writing. Occasionally, students formed small groups to work on a specific project during either the second or the last part of the period; at these times, they were always allowed to form their own groups and work with their friends. Ms. Corvo did not use grouping by ability or achievement within the class.

The observations reported here took place during the homeroom and language arts period. Each incident that is described really happened, though not necessarily on the same day. Quotations from the speech of teachers and children, as well as descriptions of incidents, are taken directly from field notes and videotapes. A major purpose of this chapter is to give the reader a context in which to understand the analysis chapters that will follow. Therefore, I have deliberately included in this account some incidents that appear in those chapters, hoping to make a strong link for the reader between analysis and context.

A Typical Language Arts Period.   It is a Thursday morning, and by 8:15, most of the students in Ms. Corvo's room are in their seats. Sean is turned around in his seat talking to Hugh, who sits behind him. Andrew and Adam are deeply engaged in a discussion of the horror movie they saw on Sunday. Some of the other students are also chattering, but Donny, James, and Kim are sitting silently in their seats.

The voice of the PA system is heard in the room, telling students and teachers which buses are late and what clubs will meet during the after-school activity period the next day. The voice ends by telling everyone to have a good day, and as it dies away Ms. Bridgestone moves to the front of the room and stands next to the front science table, slightly to one side of the center of the room.

"Please get out your paper for the practice spelling test. You should already have numbered your papers 1 to 20."

Two students go to the pencil sharpener.

"All pencils should have been sharpened during homeroom," she notes.

She waits while students retrieve spelling papers from desks and notebooks.

"Andrew, this is not a time to talk."

Ms. Bridgestone walks down the center aisle, leaning over to speak to one or two students whose papers are not ready. Returning to the front of the room, she says, "All right, put up your barriers."

Those students who have not already done so, set up a large dictionary so that it stands between them and the student in the next desk.

Ms. Bridgestone walks over and adjusts the "barrier" between Hugh and Donald. These two boys are friends, and each of them usually sits at a desk isolated from the rest of the students. As an experiment, Ms. Bridgestone is letting them sit together this morning, and she is aware of a potential for problems.

"I am ready to begin," she says, using a very calm, firm tone of voice.

The students respond instantly and sit silently, pencils poised over papers, eyes on Ms. Bridgestone.

"OK, the first word is *relax*. After school I like to relax."

Every student is quiet, focused on writing the spelling word. This is a time when everyone is very clear on what he or she is supposed to be doing. They move smoothly through the spelling list. Ms. Bridgestone is watching to make sure she is not going too fast for them to keep up, and to see which students may be missing a word that she should repeat. During word 16, the PA system interrupts, calling for another teacher to come to the office.

Soon they have reached the twentieth and last word. Lewis gets up and goes to the pencil sharpener.

"No, Lewis, not now."

He goes back to his seat with a disgusted look.

"Are there any words you want to me to repeat?"

Three hands go up.

"Those of you who have all the words, go back and check your spelling and your handwriting."

LaToya asks, "What is number 17?"

Ms. Bridgestone repeats the word. She responds to the other two students who have raised their hands, and then says, "Lewis? Did you need a word?"

Though he has not raised his hand, he asks for number 6. "I noticed that he was looking confused during the test, and I thought he must have missed a word," she says later.

Because this is a practice test, the students will check their own papers. Ms. Bridgestone reminds them to make a list of the words they missed, "so you can be responsible for studying only the ones you need to."

"Let's go through these quickly," she says.

She calls on a student to spell each of the words. Most are spelled correctly, especially because Ms. Bridgestone (as she told me in an interview) makes a point of calling on the less able students to spell the easiest words. She repeats each correct spelling in a clear voice so all can hear. "Some of them don't speak very loudly," she says later.

Hugh misspells his word, and Ms. Bridgestone prompts him, "You only left out one letter. Say it again, you know it."

Now, he spells the word correctly. She repeats his spelling and goes on.

She walks over to Lewis and asks him if he is writing down the words he needs to study. "He wasn't doing it," she said later. "I reminded him to, but

I didn't push it. It would just have been a big struggle, and we didn't need to take time to do that."

"This list was not too difficult. How many students already have 100 on it?"

About half of the hands go up. "Good. OK, put the paper in the spelling section of your notebook and don't forget to study the words you missed for the test on Friday. Kathy, will you hand out these worksheets?"

Kathy gets up and hands them out; Ms. Bridgestone goes over to where Hugh and Donald are sitting and speaks quietly to them. Lewis gets up and goes to the pencil sharpener. He sharpens, empties the sharpener into the wastebasket, sharpens some more. He takes a long time to return to his seat.

The next activity is one that Ms. Bridgestone has used once before during her stay in the classroom. On a worksheet is a list of vocabulary words taken from the novel the students are reading. Each word is given in the sentence in which it appears in the book. The students are to guess the meaning of the word from its context, write that down, and then look up the word in the dictionary, copy its definition, and compare their guess with the dictionary meaning. The purpose of the activity, as Ms. Bridgestone explains to the students, is to help give them confidence in their own ability to get the meaning of a word from context as they read, so that they will not give up when they find unfamiliar words in a book they are reading.

Her plan is to go over a few of the words as a group and then give the students time to work independently on the rest of the list. She begins to talk, stops and waits a few seconds until everyone is quiet, then begins again.

When she has reviewed the directions with the students, she reads the first sentence on the list: "Their friendship was sealed together by a mutual loss." "What do you think *mutual* might mean?"

Andrew raises his hand, is called on, and gives a definition. Ms. Bridgestone calls on several others who add their similar guesses to Andrew's. Some of the students seem really involved in this activity—it's clear they view it as a kind of game in which they are trying to outguess the dictionary.

She calls on Donald, who has looked up the word in the dictionary. The definition he reads is very close to the ones they have been giving. On the second word, Keiyon, who is sitting in the back of the room, has his dictionary in his lap and looks up the word without being seen by Ms. Bridgestone. He raises his hand, is called on, and gives the dictionary definition.

"Very good, Keiyon."

When they have reviewed the first two words orally, she tells the students they have 10 minutes to work individually on the assignment. Everyone settles right down to work. Ms. Bridgestone circulates around the room, stopping first at Rosie's desk, though she has not asked for help. Next, she helps Kathy, who has her hand up, and then walks over to June, one of the weaker students in the class. They smile very sweetly at one another. Later, Ms. Bridgestone says, "There are certain ones that I always need to check on, just to make sure they understand what's going on."

Donald raises his hand and calls softly, "Ms. Bridgestone." She goes to help him.

Now, Ms. Bridgestone goes over to Lewis and finds that he does not have a worksheet. She gets him one, and he begins to write.

After a few moments, she tells the students to put the worksheets away in their notebooks. "You can work on them between 11:45 and 12 after lunch, so you won't need to have them as homework. Now get out your *Cybil War* [the novel they are reading]. We're on page 102."

Student voices are heard. "98? What page? What page did you say we're on? Did we have this for homework?" Ms. Bridgestone ignores them.

Meanwhile, the students put away the worksheets and get out their books. Some of them quietly move into vacant desks near the front of the room or carry their chairs up to fill in the center aisle. They have been doing this for the past few weeks so that everyone can hear better during oral reading. As Ms. Bridgestone mentioned earlier, not everyone reads very loudly; almost no one reads with much expression.

When all the students are in their places and are silent, Ms. Bridgestone says, "Yesterday with our partners we read 'An Hour of Misfortune'. What was that about, for the people who weren't here yesterday?"

Hugh raises his hand to answer and gives a good summary of the chapter. It ends with the main characters making plans for a movie date.

"What do you think is going to happen on this date?" Ms. Bridgestone asks.

Many of the students have ideas, and she records them on the chalkboard, though she does not write down the silliest ones. There is a lot of enthusiasm, and when the noise gets too loud, Ms. Bridgestone shushes them—not crossly, but just to keep the noise down so they can continue.

Hugh says something, and she says, "Hugh, what was that? That was a good comment."

Hugh repeats his comment and looks pleased.

When the chalkboard is full, she begins to read at the beginning of the chapter. She says later that she did this to get the reading off to a good start "and to settle them down, too." Hugh says something and Ms. Bridgestone stares at him while continuing to read.

Finishing a paragraph, she calls on James to read. He reads in a very soft voice, but reads correctly. While James is reading, Ms. Bridgestone leans over to show Marlon the correct page to be on. "Thank you, James," she says, and looks at Donald.

"Will you read, Donald?"

Donald takes a minute to find his place; later, Ms. Bridgestone says that she called on him because she saw he was not paying attention. He reads with some hesitation. While he is reading, Ms. Bridgestone moves to the back of the room. Without a word, and without even catching Keiyon's eye, she removes from his hands an origami crane he is playing with.

When Donald finishes a paragraph, Ms. Bridgestone says, "Thank you, Donald."

He goes right on reading.

LaToya, who is sitting behind him, whispers fiercely, "She said you could stop."

Donald stops at the end of a sentence.

"Rosie?" says Ms. Bridgestone.

Rosie reads with great difficulty, stumbling over many of the words. When she reads "taking" for "talking," LaToya says quietly, "Talking." Rosie corrects herself and goes on. A few sentences later, Andrew helps her in the same way.

"Thank you, Rosie," says Ms. Bridgestone. "Paul, will you read?"

Paul reads with some expression. No one helps him when he stumbles.

Ms. Bridgestone calls on Marie next, and after her turn they stop to talk about what is going on in the book. Students join in this brief discussion without raising their hands.

Ms. Bridgestone says, "Kathy has her hand up," but Kathy says she only wanted a turn to read. After one or two more comments, Ms. Bridgestone calls on Kathy, who begins to read.

LaToya gets the next turn, and pauses, struggling with the word *pessimistically*. Ms. Bridgestone interrupts, asking the class what the word means. No one seems to know, and she supplies the definition. LaToya goes on with her turn. Most of the students seem to be on task, but Peter stretches hard and starts playing with his hair.

Ms. Bridgestone says, "Thank you, LaToya," and adds, "Let's stop for a minute and ask what did Simon find out on this infuriating date that was very surprising?"

She says later that she herself found this part of the plot very confusing, so she figured they probably didn't understand it either. Andrew gives a long and basically correct response to the question, clarifying who said what to whom and why. Ms. Bridgestone adds some comments about his response.

Donald and Hugh are talking to each other. She asks who would like to read next.

As she speaks, Andrew comments softly, "I would never act like that." He is referring to the characters in the novel, but his reaction appears to go unheard.

Lewis gets up and packs his backpack. He is going for his first session with the learning disabilities teacher. Ms. Corvo goes over to him, helps him get his things together, and they leave the room. No one seems to pay attention to this, or to see it as other than routine.

Andrew finishes reading the chapter. A discussion involving most of the students begins. They go over the list of predictions to see which ones are correct. There is a lot of laughter about the ones that were far off the mark.

Ms. Bridgestone very dramatically reads the title of the last chapter. Paul and two other students have reading turns.

Thomas turns around to talk to Andrew, and Ms. Bridgestone says softly, "Tho-o-omas." He turns forward, but a minute later he turns back to Andrew to finish his sentence. Ms. Bridgestone begins to read. Hugh is whispering to Donald, and she says, "Hugh." Hugh stops whispering.

The end of the book is approaching, and all the students seem to be absorbed in it, although Andrew and Joann are twitching their legs under their desks. One of the students makes a comment while Ms. Bridgestone is reading, and she laughs and raises her eyebrows. Later, she says that she chose to read for two reasons. They were running out of time for the lesson and she thought that if she read, it would be easier for the students to enjoy the ending of the book. It is clear to her and to me that the difficulty some students have with reading aloud impedes the others' enjoyment of the novel.

They reach the last words of the book. Most of the students seem attentive. Darin, Hugh, Donald, and Kim are not looking at their books, but are quiet and seem to be listening.

Ms. Bridgestone asks, "How would you rate that book on a scale of 1 to 10?" Many voices answer, "10, 9, 9, 5, 8.5, 6." She flips the light switch off. There is only one small window in the back of the room; whenever she does this the room seems inky black for a moment.

It is precisely 9:00 when she flips the switch back on and says, "Put away your chairs and get ready for a mini-lesson. This better not take you guys forever." They move back to their seats.

"Good," she says. "Most of you got back quickly."

She tells the class that they have only 3 weeks left before they receive their interim grades. Near the end of the interim period, she tells them they will each select their one best piece of writing completed so far during the grading period and be graded on that one.

"That will be your grade for the interim report cards."

"What's an interim?" someone says, but there is no response.

Today they will begin by reviewing the steps of writing workshop because they have been working on something else for a while.

She asks, "What are the steps of writing workshop?" There is a poster on the wall listing these steps, but neither she nor the students refer to it or look at it during the following discussion. They proceed through the steps, as a student names each one and Ms. Bridgestone expands on the idea.

"OK," says Ms. Bridgestone, "since so many of you will be starting new pieces today, let's share our ideas for our pieces. Who would like to be first?"

Quickly erasing their predictions about the movie date, she writes the students' ideas as they call them out. Andrew raises his hand and says that he wants to write about drugs and gangs in Los Angeles. Many of the ideas are about crime, drugs, and horror movies. Ms. Bridgestone later says that she is concerned about the heavy emphasis on these topics in their writing, but she accepts the ideas they put forward.

Students are calling out with some excitement, and commenting on one another's ideas. Each time Ms. Bridgestone turns around to write an idea on the board, the noise level rises. All the talk, though, seems to be about the writing ideas.

Peter turns around and is looking at Andrew. Ms. Bridgestone says, "Peter, turn around and put your feet under your desk. It will help to keep you from talking."

Peter says, "I wasn't talking."

"I know," she says, "but it will help you not to talk anymore." Peter turns around.

Ms. Bridgestone is bothered more and more by the noise level. She says "Shhhh" several times, flips the lights off once, and finally asks loudly for quiet.

Silence falls, and she says, "OK, who needs to conference?" LaToya and Joann raise their hands.

"OK, LaToya and Joann, I'm going to put a time limit on your conference, so be efficient. You can have seven minutes."

LaToya and Joann go to conference in the space behind the file cabinet.

Ms. Bridgestone asks, "OK, who wants to go to No Man's Land?" (This is Ms. Corvo's name for the spaces between the science tables.)

Paul and Kathy raise their hands.

"OK," says Ms. Bridgestone. She restates the rules for being in No Man's Land: "But you have to stay there the whole period, and no talking to anyone. Everyone else should be writing." The room is very quiet.

Ms. Bridgestone goes over to Peter and tells him that if he wants to conference he should raise his hand and she will find him someone to conference with. The noise level begins to rise. Paul, who is in No Man's Land, is talking to Andrew, who is at his nearby desk. Ms. Bridgestone is talking to Terrell. Darin goes over to the publishing center to put his finished piece in a binding.

Hugh is not working. Ms. Corvo notices this and sends him to his isolated seat. He says he can't think of anything to write; she suggests that he make a list of ideas.

Paul and Andrew are talking again; no one seems to notice. Ms. Bridgestone sees that Donald is out of his seat, and calls out, "Donald, Donald, in your seat." He sits down.

She goes to the back of the room and talks quietly with Ms. Corvo. Now Adam, Darin, and Keiyon are talking. Hugh turns around to talk to Simone and Marie, who have been writing together. Andrew goes over to Ms. Corvo and asks her for the spelling of a word. Kathy, who was in No Man's Land, is now at the front of the room talking to Joann.

Darin, one of the lowest achieving and most frequently tuned out students in the class, comes up to Ms. Bridgestone and shows her his cover with glue-and-glitter letters that he made in the publishing center. She praises it and tells him that she would never be able to make such a neat one because she has trouble with the glue.

Ms. Corvo calls Marlon over to show her what he has written today. He has nothing to show, and she scolds him at length for not working. Andrew asks Ms. Corvo for the spelling of a word. Donald is talking to Thomas.

Although few of the students work steadily through the period, all but Hugh and Marlon have done some writing, and the room does not get really noisy. The noise seems to come in surges, rising and then falling as more students settle to their work.

At 9:45, the bell rings, signalling that they have 5 minutes to get ready to leave for their next class. Ms. Corvo says, "OK, everybody in their seats. 1–2–3."

When all are in their seats, Ms. Corvo praises them for working well. She goes to the back of the room to get something, and at once they start to fool around. Walter and Terrell are dueling with their pencils. LaToya is punching Walter.

The bell rings at 9:50, and Ms. Corvo says loudly, "Alrighty. OK, guys, chairs under the desks."

They charge out noisily, her voice echoing after them, urging them to leave the room neat.

* * *

In what ways is this a language arts period typical of those I saw in Ms. Corvo's classroom? First, it follows the standard pattern for those periods. Week in and week out, most language arts periods have this same shape: spelling (or vocabulary), round-robin reading, teacher-led language arts activity, and writer's workshop. Second, although the teachers have carefully organized time and space to control student behavior, I observed many instances of students offering at least some resistance to the teacher's plans.

It wasn't clear how much academic learning was happening in Ms. Corvo's classroom. I often saw students who seemed to be off task, but I know that students can be listening and learning when they don't appear to be. It was the activities themselves that seemed to have little to offer the students in terms of learning. Day after day, they spent long stretches of time on the round-robin reading, in which each student had very little time to engage in actual reading. The amount of writing that actually got done in writer's workshop was small; few of these students seemed to take off in their writing as I have seen happen in other classrooms. Following procedures and controlling the amount of student interaction seemed to have become the primary agenda in this classroom.

Ms. Corvo explained why this was so. She had tried, she said, the kinds of activities she had done at her previous school, but they had not succeeded with these low-achieving students. Like the teachers studied by Sarason (1990), she had defined her role in the classroom as one of keeping order, and she believed that students could not learn if order was not maintained. Therefore, she believed by keeping the classroom orderly, she was creating an environment in which at least some learning could take place—even if she then could not provide what she thought were better learning activities. Was she right? I have no answer to this question. I did not see the kinds of student behavior that had led her to abandon a more varied and less controlled menu of classroom activities. I had no opportunity to see her try anything but the kind of teaching to which she had resigned herself—for this year, anyway.

Chapter 4

Sue Anderson's Fifth-Grade Classroom: A Sample Language Arts Period

૪૦ ◆ ૦ઢ

Sue Anderson's large classroom is full of light on this December afternoon. Twenty-two fifth graders sit at desks arranged in small clusters as
they discuss three questions they've answered about a novel they are
reading, *Maniac Magee*. Two of the groups are arguing about the third
question: Is *color-blind* a good word to describe Maniac (the novel's
protagonist)? Why? Most of the students agree that the question is about
Maniac's vision, his ability to see color. Some say no, he wasn't color-
blind. There wasn't anything in the book about his not being able to see
colors. Some say color-blind means you can't see any colors, only black
and white, like old movies on TV. A few have the idea that the question
refers to race. Ms. Anderson, who has been walking around the room,
listening in on the groups' discussions, asks Kelly to read aloud the place
where Maniac reveals he doesn't know the difference between the West
End and the East End. Maniac tells someone that he (a White child) lives
in the Black neighborhood. Actually, he is homeless.

Yuri, an Israeli boy, raises his hand and gives an example from Israeli
history of sabras (native-born Israelis) mistreating immigrants. Then he
states the exact meaning of color-blind in the context of the book. There
is a buzz of talk at the clusters of desks as students make connections and
share them with others. Ms. Anderson waits for this chatter to subside.
"Now," she says, "what would it be like if we were all color-blind here?"

THE COMMUNITY

Greentree School, where Sue Anderson teaches, is part of a school system serving two suburban towns, Riverland and Quiet Lawn. Riverland, a town of 14,000, is adjacent to a large city in the Midwest. Some of Riverland's neighborhoods are solidly middle class and White; others are working class and more racially diverse. It is one of only a few suburbs of the large city that possesses significant racial diversity. Riverland includes several large county parks, as well as an area set aside for light industry and a shopping strip that includes a large indoor mall and many clusters of shops and restaurants.

Quiet Lawn, which is much smaller than Riverland in size and population and does not abut on the city, is a wealthy enclave. It is carefully zoned to permit the building of none but expensive houses on large lots. A few smaller houses from the past remain, but they also sell for relatively high prices. It is likely that many of the children who live in Quiet Lawn attend private schools; in fact, the suburb is home to the most prestigious private school in the urban area and has no public school. However, Greentree School is in the part of Riverland that is closest to Quiet Lawn, and those Quiet Lawn students who do attend public elementary school go there.

Because the Riverland–Quiet Lawn district is in the county that includes the city, it is part of a voluntary integration program through which students of color from the city can attend suburban schools, and White students from the suburbs can attend school in the city. Some city families participate in this program because they believe their children will receive a superior education in the suburbs. Some White suburban families send their children to the city's magnet schools, which are far more varied than River-land–Quiet Lawn's two elementary schools, and which offer a more racially diverse experience that is attractive to some parents.

Other families send children to the city for exceptional education services or other alternative offerings provided by the city for its larger population. In addition, the district belongs to a consortium with other suburban districts through which many students with special needs receive services at just one school. Children with learning and emotional disabilities are served at Greentree School, as well as a few children with other disabilities whose parents want their children to be included in their neighborhood school.

Riverland has in recent years attracted a number of recent immigrant families from many parts of the world, including the Near East, Southeast Asia, India, and Russia. Along with the African-American, Latino, and Asian children who live in Riverland or travel from the city, these children contribute to a far more diverse ethnic makeup than that of most other noncity schools in the urban area, though White children are still a substantial majority.

The Riverland–Quiet Lawn system includes only kindergarten through eighth grade; when they reach ninth grade, students attend a highly competitive and well-funded high school with its own superintendent and school board. The high school takes in students from two other small districts, both middle class and White in population.

Because of the relatively high income levels in Riverland and Quiet Lawn, schools in this district are more luxurious than many others in the urban area; compared with almost any schools in the United States, they are spacious, pleasant, and well-maintained, and provide many amenities for students.

THE SCHOOL

Greentree School is a sprawling one-story building set well back from a busy street behind a row of houses and some public tennis courts. A central entrance area includes the office, the multipurpose room (cafeteria, gym, and auditorium), the library, and small rooms for exceptional education resource teachers. (There are no self-contained exceptional education rooms; Riverland–Quiet Lawn has been practicing a limited form of inclusion for many years.)

To the right is a large wing that serves students in Grades K through 3; to the left, a smaller wing has space for fourth- and fifth-grade classrooms. In the large wing is a computer lab with over 30 Macintosh computers and a highly qualified full-time aide. In the smaller wing are a music room and an art room, both large and well equipped.

The hallways in the central section are lined with colorful and well-executed art projects, and windows in the central hallway look out onto an area where students in a previous year created a natural area as part of an ecology project. Hallways in the two wings hold individual lockers for each student. At the far end of each of the wings are doors opening onto a large blacktop play space and beyond it, a grassy area. Students go through these doors to outdoor recess twice a day, weather permitting.

The school has a friendly atmosphere, and seems to be a place where most teachers and children get along well. Tensions around contract bargaining between the school board and teachers were high during the time I was visiting the school, and teachers sometimes spoke cynically about that situation. Relationships among teachers, however, were mostly positive. The principal expected teachers at the same grade level to work in tight-knit teams, and she contributed to making that happen. Negative interactions within a team might lead to someone's being moved to a different grade level and a new team. I had little contact with the principal, but Sue Anderson and other teachers generally spoke of her in a positive way. Among other things, she urged teachers to participate in peer-coaching relationships, and Sue Anderson considered such a relationship a positive experience.

THE CLASS

The year I was at the school, there were three fifth-grade homerooms (some years there would be two fifth grades and a 4–5 combination), and Sue Anderson's class was one of them. The children were heterogeneously grouped in the three homerooms, where they had science and social studies as well as guidance activities (the school had a full-time guidance counselor). For math and reading, about a third of the children had been identified as high academic achievers, and went together to one of the classrooms for instruction; the remaining students were divided evenly between the other two rooms. Ms. Anderson did not teach a high academic group, perhaps because she was new to the team; she had previously been teaching these groups in the fourth grade. In an interview with her, I said I had noticed that when she was talking with the class, almost all her questions were what are called high-level questions; she seldom asked a recall question. She responded:

> I'm used to working with HAS [high academic] kids [in fourth grade] and I don't teach very differently with these kids.... Maybe these kids are heterogeneous, but they don't feel different from HAS. Maybe their answers are a bit less involved, but they are thinking in that way.

I was an observer in Ms. Anderson's room over the course of the year at almost all times of the day and saw homeroom, science, social studies, computer, reading, and math classes. There were about 20 students in each class, and the composition of the class varied only slightly for the different subjects (reading, math, and homeroom classes). In reading class, for example, there were 10 boys and 10 girls. Four students were African-American, including three boys and a girl, and there was one Latino boy and one Asian girl. Fourteen of the students were White.

Students whose families came from other countries and who were in at least one of the three groupings included a boy and a girl from India, two girls from Iran, a boy from Russia, a boy from Israel (his parents were temporarily in the United States, and they returned to Israel after the winter holidays), and a boy from Vietnam. Of these, the girl from India, one of the girls from Iran, and the boy from Israel were in Sue Anderson's reading group. This meant that almost half the students in the reading class were not from American-born White families. There were two students, both White girls, who were from working-class backgrounds; one was in all three groups with Sue Anderson, whereas the other working-class girl was only in the math group.

Two students—one of the White working-class girls and one of the African-American boys—were designated as learning disabled and received resource services, but they were in Sue Anderson's room most of the day. One other African-American boy received extra support from the reading teacher for specific difficulties he had in reading, and one of the White boys received help from the guidance counselor because of emotional difficulties; neither of these children was labeled as having a disability.

The Teacher

Sue Anderson, unlike Ms. Corvo with her student teacher and Ms. Kaminski with the various adults who were part of her classroom, worked alone with her class of fifth graders. This teacher, with 20 years of classroom experience, has an almost elfin face, a crop of short, reddish hair, and a wiry body well-suited to her interest in athletics—cross-country skiing, motorcycling, rollerblading. Married with two daughters, she had taught at Greentree School for about 10 years.

The year I observed her classroom was her first as part of the fifth-grade team after teaching fourth grade for some years. She is a soft-spoken woman, serious, but with a ready sense of humor and a gentle manner. As a teacher she focused on positive interactions with the children, and on what she called sharing control with them. She told me, though, that this style represented a real change in her way of teaching. Before the previous year, she said, "I was very different ... much more controlled. I didn't give the kids that much leeway .... it was more like 'you speak when you are spoken to'."

She was pleased with this change in her teaching because, she said, "[I am] not so tired at the end of a day .... I don't feel I have to be in control of my class at all times, ... but the children and I are partners in making our classroom work."

Ms. Anderson had made a conscious decision to change her teaching and was very much aware of her daily actions in the classroom as she tried to act on that decision. She commented on how important it was to her to use what she called positive language and actions, both with the children in her class and with colleagues and family. She said:

> It was very easy for me to think about why I didn't like something or why a child shouldn't be doing something and comment on that. I'm happy [because] we seem to be accomplishing so much more during the day. We have our off days but we seem to be able to work though problems a lot easier than in the past.

Another part of the shift in Ms. Anderson's teaching was her introduction of goal-setting activities in her classroom. She described this process in a paper she wrote in graduate school:

After the children had a chance to become familiar with their classroom, goals were generated through student discussion of the question, "If you had the opportunity to create an ideal classroom, what would it look like, keeping in mind that you are here to learn?" .... [Their answers] became the classroom goals .... The class worked together to achieve these goals, which fell into the four categories of Getting Along with Others, Listening to Each Other, Being Responsible, and Respecting Each Other. Each category was defined in terms of the specific actions by students and teacher that would "look like" the overall goal. Reminding and complimenting each other and the teacher became a regular part of classroom life.

As a fifth-grade teacher, Sue Anderson had to work with a complex curriculum, and was concerned about the children's success when they moved on to middle school the next year. One of the first things she told me when I began to observe her class was that she felt "pinched" by the time constraints that were built into the fifth-grade experience at Greentree School—children had many special classes, guidance classes, and music lessons. And she was also restricted by various administrative requirements, such as giving unit tests from the basal series and placing them in the students' cumulative folders, with an eye to their grouping in middle school.

Possibly one reason she felt so restricted was that—at least at this moment in her teaching career—she had such a strong focus on the students' interaction with her and with one another. This sometimes made the content curriculum seem to be only a vehicle for what she wanted the children to learn about how to live together in the classroom and how to learn.

Nevertheless, Ms. Anderson did stick closely to the prescribed curriculum in many ways. Although the fifth-grade team rarely brought its students together as a group for any kind of instruction, the three teachers did meet and plan together. All the fifth-grade students engaged in activities such as writing a research paper and a five-paragraph essay, carrying out an end-of-year activity of painting plywood tables for the classrooms with scenes from Native-American history and practicing and reenacting a Revolutionary War battle. They moved through prescribed math units, took the basal unit tests in reading, learned spelling words, and studied pre-Colonial, Colonial, and Revolutionary War America in social studies and the ecology of wetlands and other common topics in science.

However, Ms. Anderson, who was an experienced teacher with a seemingly infinite fund of instructional ideas, built on the basis of this curriculum a classroom in which two watchwords were *variety* and *choice*. (Kounin, 1970, described variety as the first of five classroom arrangements that promote teacher control.) When it was time for spelling practice, children chose who they would work with, in what part of the room, and using what methods—spelling the words aloud to one another, writing them on a chalkboard, slate, or paper, or making up mnemonics to help them remember. They frequently moved their desks into new arrangements. Sometimes they read from stories the class had selected from their basal reader and at other times from paperback novels. When they were studying Indian nations, they could choose a nation that interested them, be grouped with others who had made the same choice, and then choose one or more ways of expressing what they learned from a list of over 50 possibilities. In my descriptions of Ms. Kaminski's and Ms. Corvo's classrooms, I wrote about a *typical* day; in describing Ms. Anderson's classrooms I had to write about a *sample* day, because there was so little consistency in the activities I observed over the course of the year. The children seemed to thrive on this diet of variety and choice.

The Classroom's Appearance

The first thing I noticed on entering Sue Anderson's fifth-grade classroom was how large it was. Her suburban school was built with an eye to spaciousness. In fact, 60 fifth graders attended a video showing in a similar classroom. They were sitting on all the chairs, on the carpet, and on the counters that ran under the windows and across the back of the room, but the room seemed full, not crowded. The spaciousness of Ms. Anderson's room meant that it never seemed cluttered or crowded, even when a great deal was going on in the room. This spaciousness made it easier to arrange and rearrange Ms. Anderson's room, which contained about 25 lightweight desks and chairs, a teacher's desk, three round tables, and a Danish-style couch, as well as bookcases and built-in counters. Ms. Anderson and her students rearranged this furniture often. Her teacher desk and storage shelves were much the heaviest pieces of furniture in the classroom, and they were permanently located in one corner of the room. In addition, the room was carpeted, and students often sat on the carpet, gathering in groups in open areas, or finding a place to work alone—next to, or even under, desks or tables.

Starting at the door from the hallway, a chalkboard ran almost all the way across the room to the left. In the corner was Ms. Anderson's desk, which seemed to serve mainly as a place to deposit papers and books. I saw her sit at it only once during the year, and she explained that she was tired from not sleeping well the night before. In front of the desk was an overhead projector, bins for recycling paper of various kinds, and crates to hold needed materials. At times, there was also a cart full of books from the library on some topic the class was working on. Behind the desk were storage shelves for Ms. Anderson's books and papers and a bulletin board where she posted notices or plans she wanted to remember.

The next wall was made of north-facing windows, looking out on grass and trees. Below them was a counter topping radiators and bookshelves; one held the class collection of games for use when rain or cold required indoor recess. In the spring, crickets and chameleons lived in cages on the counter. The third wall had a large bulletin board, where student work was always posted, and another long counter with storage shelves below. Here were the classroom computer, baskets for turning in work for various subjects, supplies of paper, a sink, and a drinking fountain. The fourth wall, backing on the hallway, had another bulletin board, a smaller chalkboard, and a tall bookcase holding the classroom library.

The Daily Schedule

The children who were in Sue Anderson's homeroom group began the day with her at 9:00. Some of them had already attended a Spanish or French language class before school; it met 2 days a week and was available to students whose parents paid a fee and brought them to school early. Homeroom was a time to hear announcements and to talk about upcoming events; once a week they had a kind of show-and-tell time, in which children could tell about something they thought would interest the class. This also was the time when the guidance counselor would come in to teach conflict resolution, problem solving, and the like. At the end of Homeroom, the students had a brief Daily Oral Language lesson, in which a sentence containing errors in grammar, usage, or mechanics was written on the board and the students offered oral corrections and took turns writing them in.

At 9:30, they would usually go to physical education, music, or art, returning at 10:15 for math class. Not all Ms. Anderson's homeroom students were in her math class; some went to one of the other teachers for what was called HAS math, for high ability students. One of the few predictable activities of the day occurred at the beginning of math class; as each student came in, Ms. Anderson or a student she had asked to help would hand each child a slip of paper with four or five review problems, and that was the first thing to be done. This seemed to settle the students after the transition; nearly all could do these problems correctly.

The class would quickly exchange and correct these papers and pass them in; then they would correct their homework if it had been assigned. Sometimes the math homework would just be to correctly complete any problems missed on the previous homework, and those papers would be turned in without further correction. The remainder of the math class could involve almost any kind of activity.

For some weeks in the winter, there was a running estimation contest with students bringing in a jar full of items for others to estimate how many it contained. A round-the-world game for practicing math facts was popular; students would take turns at seeing how many correct answers in a row each could get, while moving from desk to desk. Sometimes, Ms. Anderson used the overhead projector to explain some new or difficult concept. On other days, students gathered in groups to solve word and logic problems from a math magazine–workbook that was delivered monthly.

After math, the homeroom students returned for science class, which was followed by lunch and recess.

At 1:00, the language arts–reading period began, again with identified students attending HAS reading, and their places in Ms. Anderson's room taken by others. Here again was a moment of regularity; the first activity in reading class was spelling practice or a spelling test. This was followed by time for a wide variety of activities related to reading and language arts. The class read several novels during the year, including *Maniac Magee*, *The Sign of the Beaver*, and *My Brother Sam Is Dead*. They might gather in a large group to discuss some aspect of the novel; form small groups to answer questions posed by Ms. Anderson; make posters, mobiles, or dioramas related to their reading; or occasionally do some oral reading, although most of the reading was expected to be done at home.

At other times, they worked in the basal reader. Early in the year they read a few stories as a class, having rated the stories in the basal reader and chosen the ones they most wanted to read. This included completing related work sheets. Later, they divided a basal unit among several groups, shared what they read with one another and completed the worksheets for the unit in preparation for the required test. Other activities included creating imaginary inventions and presenting them orally to the class, creating and acting out television advertisements, playing a card game to learn prefixes and suffixes, and practicing solving analogy questions.

After reading, students from other classes left and Sue Anderson's homeroom students came back to the room for social studies. This time also included, through the year, a great variety of activities. In a major social studies unit, each student chose an Native American nation and formed a group with others with the same interest to learn and express their knowledge. At another time, as they began to talk about explorers from Europe and their activities in America, they wrote about what it would be like to be an explorer in space.

After social studies, all the fifth grades went outdoors for recess if the weather allowed; running and ball games kept most students active. When it was too cold, wet, or snowy to go out, they had indoor recess in the room, with relaxed conversation and game playing; during the winter, there was a chess tournament organized by another fifth-grade teacher.

After recess, Sue Anderson's students returned to her room for science, again a time for varied activities. One science unit involved learning about wetlands and the animals and plants that are found in such areas in their region; this culminated in a trip to a marsh. Another unit at the end of the year involved learning about the biomes they would see during a class camping trip to a local lake.

About 5 minutes before dismissal at 3:30, Ms. Anderson asked everyone to straighten up the room, check to be sure they had their homework or any notes to parents to take with them, and sent them off to the waiting buses.

In Ms. Anderson's classroom, I observed at many different times of day, throughout the school year. For the sake of consistency, I have chosen to describe a reading period in her class. This sample readers' workshop really occurred as it is described. Words of teachers and children, as well as incidents, come from field notes. To give the reader a context for understanding the analysis chapters, some incidents described here will reappear in those chapters.

A Sample Reading Period

Unlike the other two classrooms, where the structure of activities from day to day was quite predictable, Ms. Anderson's class offered different activities practically every day. The few regularities included the Daily Oral Language lesson in the morning (though I saw it postponed until the afternoon more than once), the small page of math problems (called the minisheet) handed out at the beginning of math class, and the spelling activity at the beginning of reading class. This activity did not take place every single day, but it recurred several times a week all year long. On this sample day, that was how reading period began.

The exchange of students among the fifth-grade reading classes is complete, and the boys and girls who have reading class with Ms. Anderson are sitting at their desks, which are arranged today in groups of three or four, or are milling fairly quietly around the room.

> Ms. Anderson: OK, let's study spelling words. Remember, you set your goal for the number you hoped to spell correctly this week. Let's get in pairs and choose the way you will study today.

Three pairs of girls go to the chalkboard, while other pairs are reading the words to each other. Two pairs include both a boy and a girl. Dara needs an eraser, and she comes over to the small chalkboard, where Kerri and Karen are practicing together, and picks one up.

> Karen: Excuse me, Dara, we are using that. [This is an exceptionally rude comment to hear in this classroom, especially since there are three identical erasers on the chalk rail.] Dara silently picks up a different eraser.

After about 10 minutes of practice time, the rest of the reading period begins with an activity for the whole class that involves defining words in a Native-American language found in the book *The Sign of the Beaver*. This novel tells the story of a young boy, Matt, who is left to care for his family's newly built cabin in the woods while the father travels to get his mother and the younger children. The boy's rifle and food supplies are stolen by a traveler, leaving him in considerable danger. He is helped by an older

Native-American man, who asks the boy to teach English to his grandson Atean, believing that it will be helpful to him in the future. After considerable conflict between the two boys, they reach a state of uneasy friendship, in which each learns from the other. The father returns, and the Native Americans move away.

There are eight vocabulary words on the list. Everyone seems to be tuned in as they locate the words in their individual copies of the novel and use context clues to figure out the meanings. This is not too difficult, and most of the answers are right on the first try. Yet, Stephen, who Ms. Anderson has told me is identified as having a learning disability, does give a wrong response for the last word. He defends his answer, saying that the book gives his answer in another place.

> Ms. Anderson (politely): Well, Stephen, you find that place in your book, and tell us when you find it. OK?

My impression is that she is quite sure that he is wrong. He starts to flip through the pages, but stops as soon as she begins to give their assignment for the next day. As homework, they are supposed to write an answer to this question:

> Ms. Anderson: What you can do is, pretend that there is a new child in our classroom who doesn't speak any English. What would you do to help that child learn English? Let's take a few minutes to brainstorm some ideas ....

Hands go up right away. After each response, Ms. Anderson says "Good," "Nice idea," "Good idea," "Nice thinking."

> Karen: Use a beginner dictionary, with pictures.
> Joshua: Teach the letter sounds.
> William: Have them look at sentences.
> Mike: Get an interpreter who can speak both languages.
> Terry: Use an ABC picture book.
> Ms. Anderson: You mean, you could show them the pictures and say the words.
> Kevin: You could have them copy letters.
> Shonda: You could point to stuff in the room and say the name of it real slowly. Then you could have them repeat it after you.
> Darren: You could teach the numbers.
> Stephen: You could get a library book in English and use it to teach the colors.
> Shonda: You could get a library book that's in both languages.

During this discussion, most have been paying attention and eagerly raising their hands to participate. Terry has been drawing, and Michelle is out of her seat and moving around. Kerri and Karen, who are sitting together, are both involved in drawing and looking to see what the other is doing. As usual, Ms. Anderson ignores these (relatively few) off-task activities that don't seem to interfere with others.

> Ms. Anderson: Now, if you had to choose just one of these good ideas, which one would work best for you?
> Vincent: Get a translator.
> Denny: Sound out the letters.
> Craig: Use pictures.
> Ms. Anderson: OK, let's take a vote. Which do we think would be the best one? How many would learn quicker with pictures?

Over half the hands go up.

> Ms. Anderson: How many would learn best by just hearing the words?

Fewer hands go up, but Ms. Anderson has not counted and doesn't announce a result. When I asked her afterward why she didn't, she said that most of the answers were in those two categories, and she wanted them to notice that. She added that getting an interpreter didn't really fit the question, which was, "What could you do to help?" but she didn't mention this to the children. Going on with the discussion, she said,

> Ms. Anderson: OK, so that's your homework. Now, I have some more questions. Dara, what language do you speak at home?
> Dara: Persian. We speak, you know, Persian.
> Ms. Anderson: Is any English spoken at home?
> Dara: Well, not by my parents. When I study, sometimes I translate what the book says into Persian and use a Persian dictionary.
> Yuri: We speak Hebrew at home.
> Lawrence: We speak Vietnamese. I mean, they speak it to me, I can understand it but I would never be able to say anything back to them.
> Ms. Anderson: Well, tell me this. How can you tell how a person is feeling without any words?

The answers to this question pour out so fast that I can't keep up in my notes with who is speaking. There are many references to facial expressions, complete with demonstrations of smiles, angry frowns, and tears, to tone of voice, also with demonstrations, and to actions.
Ms. Anderson affirms each of the answers.

> Ms. Anderson: OK, well, how about this. Are there signs or symbols that anyone would know, anywhere in the world?

There are no answers at all to this question, and she begins to explain about the system of international signs. She picks up a piece of chalk and draws the slashed-circle sign that means *No*.

Ms. Anderson: Are there any other signs that everyone knows?

Lawrence hurries to the board and draws a cross.

Ms. Anderson: Mmm-hmmm.

She adds the stylized wheelchair that stands for handicapped access and the male and female signs found on public bathrooms. The students don't seem to be picking up on this, and Denny and Terry are whispering, while Jennifer is using her pencil to make squeaky noises on her desk.

Ms. Anderson: Well, then, what was the sign that Atean pointed out to Matt in the book?

Many hands wave and voices call out:

Sign of the Beaver! Sign of the Turtle!

Ms. Anderson hands out a worksheet that calls for filling in the meanings of international symbols; she says that they have covered most of its contents in the discussion, and then speaks in a louder-than-usual voice:

Ms. Anderson: OK that's it, get out your assignment notebooks, please.

Most of the students comply quickly.

Ms. Anderson: I'm waiting for about half a dozen people to get their assignment notebooks out. (She waits.) OK, these are the assignments: you can write about what you would do if a child with no English came to our classroom. You can finish filling out the work-sheet on symbols. And you need to study your spelling words, because the test is tomorrow. Does everyone have that?

She turns to the door, where several children returning from another reading group are clustered.

Ms. Anderson: OK, we're finished. You can come in. We're a little late today, so please, the people from Mr. Smith's and Ms. Jones' rooms move right on out.

Quickly, students rise to their feet, gather notebooks, novels, and pencils, and move out the door or to other desks.

Although I have described this as a sample reading period, it is also typical of a reading period in Ms. Anderson's class in several ways. It is a busy, active time, with involvement in discussion by many students. It involved choices for students, this time during the spelling study period. The students' home lives were connected to the topic being discussed. As was often the case, it involved a discussion directed by Ms. Anderson. And very little time was spent on issues of discipline or management. There was little off-task behavior, and what there was, Ms. Anderson and the other students ignored.

The pleasant and cooperative atmosphere was also typical; as noted earlier, Ms. Anderson's room was characterized by a strong commitment on the part of both teacher and students to the colluded-on agenda of public courtesy. Whatever conflict there was between teacher and student agendas in this room—and there was some—it was rarely expressed overtly.

PART II

TEACHERS AND STUDENTS CONSTRUCTING POWER RELATIONS

ဢ ◆ ଔ

Chapter 5

Teachers' Organization of Time and Space: One Aspect of Classroom Power Relations

∞ ◆ ∞

In almost any classroom, an observer can watch teachers engaged in direct interaction with students that is intended to control student behavior and promote student learning. Yet, this is only one aspect of teachers' efforts to pursue this agenda. Outside the students' view, teachers plan and carry out other actions before students even come into the classroom. Thus, they contribute to the building of the structure called "What Teachers and Students Can Do Here," building walls and creating living space, without the possibility of immediate conflict with students. It is these "invisible" (Hustler & Payne, 1982) arrangements that are the focus of this chapter.

Teachers often consider the ways they organize time and space in their classrooms to be part of classroom management. Classroom management authorities call this *proactive management*, management that prevents trouble from happening, rather than dealing with it after it happens. Teachers arrange desks so they can see all the students, provide an activity for students to start on as soon as they enter the room, and leave enough space near the door for students to stand in an uncrowded line. They arrange furniture so that students have to move in a controlled manner from one area to another; they make sure they have more than enough for students to do during each class period, thus, avoiding "dead time" when trouble can occur. All these are tactics teachers use in pursuit of their agenda to control student behavior so that students can learn.

Yet, teachers may also consider arrangements of time and space in terms of curriculum content and instructional methods. They may arrange desks or replace them with tables to facilitate cooperative learning groups. They may arrange desks in rows to face the front of the room to encourage students to focus on direct instruction. A whole-language teacher may create a library area that is easily accessible to students throughout the classroom day, perhaps with comfortable seating to encourage reading; a teacher who plans to use the classroom library only as an occasional time-filler will fill a small shelf at one side of the room with tightly packed books. A teacher who regularly uses quizzes to test whether students are doing their work may arrange desks as far apart as possible to reduce opportunities for cheating. A teacher who sees the classroom day as a journey through each of the subject areas in the curriculum will create carefully structured activities that can be fitted into the time available for each subject. A teacher who plans a day centered around an integrated curriculum will arrange uninterrupted blocks of time in which extended activities can take place.

Most teachers have the prerogative of organizing classroom space—arranging desks, deciding on the use to be made of different areas, and deciding what will be kept in the classroom (within the limits of building architecture and other constraints). They also have a dominant role in deciding what kinds of activities will fill the classroom day, and often in determining how that day will be scheduled—once again, within some restrictions from the larger institution. These choices are among the most important resources teachers have as they contribute to the construction of classroom power relationships.

The idea that teachers control student actions in ways other than direct discourse is central in the literature on classroom management. Willard Waller (1932/1965), the pioneering sociologist of American education, wrote in 1932 that the teacher must have his wishes carried out, if possible, "without a direct clash of wills between teacher and student" (p. 203). He believed that ideally, the teacher would set up a permanent and unshakable power structure in the classroom: "It is better if the teacher takes the classroom situation for granted and defines the situation ... by words and deeds" (p. 305). He quoted W.C. Bagley: "The acme of good discipline is attained when the conditions of order are preserved automatically, without thought or judgement on the pupil's part" (p. 308). Despite the authoritarian vision of schooling that Waller presented, he urged that invisible regularities should be the tools of classroom management, rather than direct coercion.

More modern literature on classroom management continues the same theme. For example, Brophy (1983), writing 50 years after Waller, described the smoothly functioning classroom as one in which students display seemingly automatic orderly behavior. He viewed devoting time to management or control as an indicator of poor teaching. This idea was echoed by Morine-Dershimer (1985), who found that teachers who devote even 1% or 2% of their utterances to calls for attention are "less effective" than those who never need to seek control verbally. Doyle (1990) wrote, "Traditionally, discussions of classroom management were focused on treatment issues, that is, what to do about disruptive students or disruptive situations" (p. 352). He added that in more recent times, the focus of studies in classroom management has been on planning classroom organization to prevent disruption before it happens.

Even writers who have a much more critical approach to education see the significance of teacher choices about time and space. For example, Linda McNeil (1982), in her influential book *Contradictions of Control*, located teachers' power in their choice of instructional methods and classroom styles. What students learn in their high school economics classes, she said, depends on these teacher decisions.

In an explicit example of a teacher exercising control over the use of classroom space as a way of contributing to the construction of classroom power relations, Lampert (1985) described how, when she was faced with the problem of simultaneously controlling students' behavior and promoting gender equity in mathematics teaching, she responded by rearranging the room and reseating the students for instruction.

Oyler (1996) studied the classroom of a teacher who was, like Sue Anderson, explicit about her intention to share authority or control with her students. She observed the teacher's sharing of authority in the use of time, space, and materials.

This whole-language teacher set aside a large block of time for language-related activities, and as the year went on, it became common for students to propose, and the teacher to endorse, the order in which those activities would take place. In particular, students often called for time to write in their journals, and the teacher would agree. One of the regular activities was a teacher-led read-aloud. One day, the teacher began with this clear statement, "Remember, this is my turn to talk" (Oyler, 1996, p. 42). What actually happened was that half a dozen extended periods of student talk interrupted the read-aloud. And this was not troublesome to the teacher.

Also, the teacher Oyler observed ordinarily had student desks arranged in rows, which they could quickly rearrange into clusters for various activities. Students began to request that they write in their journals in the clusters, rather than in isolation in the rows. At first the teacher refused this request, but as it continued to be made, she agreed, even though she raised concerns with Oyler about students who did too much talking and not enough writing. In fact, just as Sunny Kaminski believed that student choices would foster learning, this teacher believed that student talk would have the same effect, so when she turned over time to students for their talk, she was in effect pursuing her own agenda of controlling student behavior to enhance student learning in that situation.

From the teacher's point of view, the advantage of using these "invisible" actions is that students will find it hard to challenge them (Hustler & Payne,

1982). Students do have ways to make these activities visible, and thus open them to challenge, as will be discussed later. But teachers have learned that these kinds of building activities are effective in promoting their own agendas.

In my work at the university level, I find myself walking into the classroom and immediately beginning to rearrange chairs and tables for the class interaction. I do this with awareness that I am contributing to building our classroom power relations in a significant way. Believing, like Sunny Kaminski and Sue Anderson, that students learn best when they have many choices, I still claim this choice as my prerogative. My understanding of the meaning and purpose of this ordinary-seeming action helps me better understand the interaction between me and my students. Like other teachers, I choose to build part of the structure of power relations before the students arrive, preempting building space before conflicts can occur.

In the three classrooms that were the focus of this study, both physical arrangements and the teachers' choice of what kinds of activities would fill the classroom day had strong effects on the actions of students. Aileen Corvo believed that students—or at least the particular group of students she was teaching—would learn best when they had little choice but to do the work she gave them. Her fifth-grade classroom was arranged so that it was hard for students to move about. They were discouraged by the room arrangement itself from directing their gaze or their attention away from the teacher standing in front of the chalkboard. In the other two classrooms, the arrangement of classroom space gave the students much more physical freedom. Like Ms. Corvo's room arrangement, this reflected Sunny Kaminski's and Sue Anderson's beliefs about student learning.

Also, in Ms. Corvo's room, as in most classrooms, teachers kept the organization of classroom time and space firmly in their own hands; Sue Anderson turned over to the students some control of the way space was used; Sunny Kaminski sometimes let students control decisions about the use of time. The three classrooms also differed in the amount of time devoted to activities to which students had a choice of many responses, as opposed to activities in which responses were strictly limited. But the choices of all three teachers, as I recognized from interviewing them and observing their classrooms, were made on the basis of their agenda of controlling student behavior to promote student learning.

PHYSICAL ARRANGEMENTS

In Aileen Corvo's fifth-grade classroom, where Courtney Bridgestone was the student teacher, the physical arrangements discouraged students both from moving around the room and from interacting with other students. In the small crowded room, desks were set close together in pairs, facing the chalkboard, on either side of a narrow aisle. At the front of the room was a small "teacher space" at the chalkboard; the room's door opened onto that space. Exit from the room was tightly controlled.

It seems unlikely that anyone could run in this space, and I never saw such a thing happen. In fact, you could only move about by picking your way slowly and carefully between the seats. Except for students in adjacent desks, conversation between students could only take place if someone turned all the way around in order to talk, or spoke across the center aisle.

Furthermore, three of the most difficult students, from Ms. Corvo's point of view, had what she called "isolated seats," which cut them off even more completely from communication with others. Hugh's desk was placed between the chalkboard and the first lab table, Lewis' between the first and second lab tables, and Donald's at the other side of the room, with his back to the rest of the students. When they were complying with the teacher's wishes, and when group instruction was taking place, the three boys were allowed to sit in vacant seats in the regular rows; if they did not comply, and during times devoted to seat work, they were sent back to their isolated seats.

Ms. Corvo had a desk at the back of the room, and she usually sat at it when Ms. Bridgestone (the student teacher) was in charge of the class. But it was clear that in this classroom the natural place for the teacher was at the front of the room.

The message Ms. Corvo's room arrangement sent was that no one needed to move, no one needed to look at anything but the front of the room, and no one needed to talk to anyone except the teacher. It was consonant with Ms. Corvo's reliance on direct instruction and teacher-led activities. This message was strikingly similar to that of an 1893 classroom described by Tyack (1974): "Children were forced to sit with eyes facing forward; even when they handed material to their neighbors, they stared 'straight in front of them', and groped sideways to pass or receive papers" (pp. 82–83).

The physical arrangement of Sunny Kaminski's first-grade classroom, on the other hand, was aimed at making possible the many choices offered there. The easel and the block play area were the only parts of the room that were not set up to permit multiple and flexible uses. No one had a desk or any permanent spot to be in at any particular time. The only sense of personal privacy was that each child had two cubbies, one for personal possessions and one for ongoing work. However, Ms. Kaminski stressed the appropriate use of the various parts of the room—the reading area for reading, the block area for block play, the tables for a variety of writing and manipulative activities, the rug (when not being used for whole-class gatherings) for reading or listening to audiotapes, and so forth.

Ms. Kaminski moved around the room during most of the day, perching on tables, pulling up chairs, and standing beside shelves. She did have a desk, but it was piled so high with books and other materials that sitting at it would have cut her off completely from the class. During sharing time, the students gathered on the rug for a joint activity—the closest they came to direct instruction. At this time, Ms. Kaminski sat in her rocking chair on the rug more often than in any other spot, but during my 14 observations of sharing time, she also sat on the table near the window, on one of the round tables near the rug, and on a child-size chair, as well as on the floor with the students. She stated clearly in several interviews that she believed that choice and flexibility actively promote learning; she provided them to control children's actions in order to promote learning. Her contribution to building power relations in the classroom included many provisions for choice by every student.

It was clear, though, that in Ms. Kaminski's room the physical arrangements were far less in conflict with student agendas of independent action than were those in Ms. Corvo's room. The contribution of her room's arrangement to the building of power relations, although real, was not as a rule an area of conflict between teacher and children. The message it sent seemed to be that there was a lot to do and a lot to choose from in the classroom, and that students were welcome to make choices.

The first thing I noticed on entering Sue Anderson's fifth-grade classroom was how large it was. This spaciousness made it easier to arrange and rearrange the room, and Ms. Anderson and her students rearranged the desks, tables, couch, and smaller bookcases at least once a month. If things were going well, it was up to the students to decide how to place the desks—in groups, circles, or rows—and where to put other furniture.

If Ms. Anderson felt that things were not going well, if she was finding it hard to get and keep the students' attention when she needed it, she might decree rows, and line up the desks in the traditional manner. This was intended, she said, as a signal to the students that she was exerting more control, even though it never seemed to interfere with individual students' regular opportunities to find a different place to work—at a table, on the couch, or at an empty desk—when they wanted to.

Through the winter months, when the weather often kept students indoors for recess, Ms. Anderson's students took weekly turns at creating a "habitat" around the Danish-style couch. Small friendship groups of two, three, or four students could use the couch and, if they chose, a couple of desks and a table, to create a "private" area. During many parts of the day, the group could work or relax in their habitat, rather than remaining at their desks or using other spaces in the room. A number of groups brought in portable stereos, though they could use them only during indoor recess or the lunch break. Two girls who were close friends brought in numerous stuffed animals, pillows, quilts, and blankets, and created a barrier of blanket-covered tables—under which they could curl up with a stuffed toy—around the couch.

After the lunch break, two or three times a week, Sue Anderson's students practiced spelling words. They formed pairs for this task, and Sue encouraged them to choose both a way of practicing and a suitable place to practice. Some pairs found a spot at one of the chalkboards and took turns writing and erasing the words. Others found a quiet corner and quizzed one another orally. Still others settled at a table, and took turns reading the words out and writing them on paper.

Sometimes, it was at Ms. Anderson's request that the arrangement of the room was changed; one day, I came in to find all the desks pushed out of the way, and the students sitting in a large circle on the carpeted floor, discussing the book they were reading as a class. Another time, the desks were in rows—her response to a piece of student misbehavior.

Ms. Anderson said she believed that students' learning is enhanced when they feel they are in control of their environment. That was why she encouraged them to make choices about the arrangement of space in the room. Although she had recently increased the amount of choice with respect to the ways of learning and expressing learning that she offered in her room, she continued to include many teacher-directed, whole-class, and nonchoice activities in the classroom day. The considerable freedom she gave students to organize space was as much a part of her agenda of control of student behavior to enhance their learning as was her demand for quiet and attention when she taught math by direct instruction, using the chalkboard and an overhead projector.

DESIGN OF ACTIVITIES

Just as teachers organize space as an "invisible resource" in their efforts to enact a classroom agenda, so they can design classroom activities to control both the visibility of their own contribution to power relations and the opportunity for student contributions. One way of doing this is to devote classroom time to activities that allow little opportunity for interaction between students to take place. Some activities of this kind that I observed were seat work (the individual completion of work sheets and the like), tests, and oral reading.

The function of these kinds of activities was most apparent in Aileen Corvo's classroom. Four mornings a week the first thing that happened in the official school day was a lesson lasting about 15 minutes (almost 15% of total language arts time for the day) that consisted of an interaction with a spelling or vocabulary list that left students with few choices of how to respond. The activity began when the teacher moved to her prescribed position for the lesson. Either Ms. Bridgestone or Ms. Corvo would move to the front of the room on the side away from the door and stand quietly. At this signal, and without a word, student bodies could be seen locking into the correct position, with feet under desks, faces to the front, hands ready to write either a test or notes, and voices silent. During this time there was little student talk, and the teacher's speech was usually restricted to repeating instructions and asking questions.

This was even more true during the spelling pretest and test. Students who sat at adjacent desks were required to take out their dictionaries and set them up as a "barrier" to prevent them from seeing the other student's work. The teacher read the list of words, and students wrote. If they missed a word, they were to wait until the list was complete to ask for a repetition.

Also, in Ms. Corvo's class, oral reading of novels by students and teacher in turn predominated in the observed lessons, with about 30% of most language arts periods devoted to it. Nearly every day, Ms. Bridgestone or Ms. Corvo said something like, "Take out your *Cybil War*. We're on page 47." Students responded to this direction not only by getting out the book and opening it to the prescribed page, but also by arranging their bodies according to the rules for oral reading. At this time they could assume some comfortable position in their seats, resting head or elbow on the desk or leaning back in the chair, but they were to face the front of the classroom, have their feet under their desks, and have their books open and their eyes on their books. One of these requirements was made explicit in this instance:

> Ms. Bridgestone: Peter, turn around and put your feet under your desk. It will help to keep you from talking.
> Peter: I wasn't talking.
> Ms. Bridgestone: I know, but it would help you not to talk any more.

Ms. Bridgestone or Ms. Corvo might stop the reading for a brief period of discussion, but the discussion could always be ended simply by saying the name of the next student to read. The end of one student's turn to read and the beginning of the next was announced with a simple "Thank you, Donald. LaToya?"

According to Ms. Corvo, this class presented severe behavior problems. She was no longer trying to carry out projects or to have several different reading groups. Instead, she had greatly increased the amount of time devoted to such activities as spelling, vocabulary, and oral reading. At these ritual times, there was rarely a need to even tell the students what to do or to correct their behavior. She had succeeded in using activities that called for strictly limited student responses to promote her agenda of student control and (she believed) enhanced learning.

In Sunny Kaminski's classroom, this teacher strategy of providing "seamless" (Griffin & Mehan, 1981) activities got very little use. Much of the day was spent in situations in which the children selected their activities, their locations, and their actions from a wide range of acceptable choices. Thus,

I could observe in her room some of the results of not providing the kinds of activities that predominated in Ms. Corvo's classroom.

When the class came together on the rug, as it did periodically throughout the day, Ms. Kaminski arranged student time in a more overtly controlled way, and certainly there were more rules. Some of these rules, as mentioned by Ms. Kaminski at various times, were:

- Be on the rug.
- Have your hands empty unless you are holding something that you will share.
- Do not sit on a chair.
- Sit up.
- Do not talk when it is someone else's turn.

According to Ms. Kaminski, she discussed these rules at length with the children in the first few days of school. However, they were far less confining than the rules for, say, oral reading in Ms. Corvo's room. Furthermore, they were constantly being broken, often, Ms. Kaminski would explain, because she thought a particular child would benefit more from breaking a rule than from keeping it. The rules did have a sort of general application, and were quoted regularly to deal with children who were interfering with the activity of the moment, but there was no sense that it was important to enforce them consistently.

As a result, when Ms. Kaminski did elect to provide an activity in which she sought to limit student responses, she had to work hard to make it happen, as in this instance from my notes:

Ms. Kaminski sits down at a table with a group of children who have been gathered there because they are those least sure of their ABC's. Each of the children has a copy of the same ABC book.

Ms. Kaminski: Please turn to the A page.

Carlton does not comply.

Ms. Kaminski: (pauses) Please turn to the A page.

Carlton continues to attend to the page he reached when he started looking through the book as soon as he sat down. Ms. Kaminski reaches over and turns his book to the page she wants him to look at. She is trying to organize a sort of round robin in which each person will read one letter and the thing it stands for in order around the table.

Ms. Kaminski: (beginning) A is for Apple.

There is quite a lot of resistance to this plan. No one seems to want to cooperate.

Ms. Kaminski: Would you like to do it [go through the ABC book] by your-
                       selves?
Voices: Yes.

Juana is going through the book. I think Jimmy may not know the letters well enough to do this on his own. Charles is rocking his chair to see if he can fall over backwards. I don't see him look at the book. But when Ms. Kaminski asks if they are finished he says yes, and she gives him and others who are finished another ABC book to look at. After a few minutes, Ms. Kaminski collects the second set of ABC books.

Ms. Kaminski: OK, now, everyone turn back to the first page and we'll sing the ABC song.

Juana is slow to turn to the right page. They go through the ABC book, singing the song.

Ms. Kaminski: Now let's go through just one more time and say it.

Now they go through the book taking turns as she first wanted them to do. Everyone is able to read her or his assigned letter and identify the related picture.

Ms. Kaminski: Good, good job, we're reading the book all the way through.

In the end, Ms. Kaminski achieved the activity she had planned, but it did not just click into place as it might have in Ms. Corvo's room. On the other hand, what substituted for it was other desirable choices (from Ms. Kaminski's point of view). This group of children needed to work on the alphabet letters, and during the activity they were engaged in various ways of learning about them. Ms. Kaminski would probably have considered the activity a success even if the last part (when the students carried out her original agenda for the group) had not happened.

This incident highlights the relationship between Ms. Kaminski's agenda for her students and her participation in building the structure of power relations in her classroom. The children here have choices, rather than being coerced by a seamless structure of events, but the choices are almost always between Ms. Kaminski's alternatives, and the choices are there precisely because Ms. Kaminski believes that children learn better when they are making choices. Ms. Kaminski has, through her planning of the day, created a structure that controls student behavior and, she believes, enhances student learning, even though it looks very different from the "seamless" structure created by Ms. Corvo.

Sue Anderson's views on the role of choice in student learning fall somewhere between those of Sunny Kaminski and Aileen Corvo. She does believe that students need to have choices, and she provides many of them in her classroom. Students begin the year by developing their goals for the classroom they would like to have, defining the actions on the part of students and teachers that will lead to those goals, and creating their own rules to encourage those actions. As discussed previously, they have many choices with regard to the use of space in the classroom. And Sue Anderson often offers a wide range of choices—for example, 50 ways to express what you learned about Native-American life—about the outcomes of the students' work or the ways they pursue it.

Yet, Ms. Anderson is a member of a team of fifth-grade teachers in a school that has a close eye on preparation for middle school and ultimately for a highly competitive high school. She sometimes resists or resents the constraints that this situation puts on her. I am in the room while Ms. Anderson is giving a basal reader unit test. She walks over to me and says:

> The only reason I give this is at the end of the year they check to see if these are in the cume [cumulative] folders. But I wonder why a test on a trade book wouldn't be acceptable. It's for the middle school, of course.

She is also perfectly willing to plan seamless, teacher-centered activities for part of the classroom time. It is by no means unusual for her to stand at the overhead projector or the chalkboard, explaining a math concept, or at the front of the classroom leading a traditional recitation session on a story the class has read.

However, variety is a major theme in Ms. Anderson's classroom. Only three times a day is there a brief activity that is repeated daily or almost daily: Students engage in the Daily Oral Language activity of correcting a sentence written on the chalkboard each morning, they have a half-sheet of math problems to do as soon as they enter math class, and they practice spelling words or take a spelling test at the beginning of the language arts period. And none of these activities involves anything like the rather rigid requirements for focus of attention and body position that are seen in Ms. Corvo's room.

Even when Ms. Anderson carries out one of her most teacher-directed activities, she is always doing something new to the group. For example, when she taught the class about angles (a review she felt they needed for a Logo activity they would be doing in the computer lab), she was using the overhead projector as a math teaching tool for one of the few times I observed during the year:

Ms. Anderson is explaining what is an acute angle using the overhead projector. She can write with chalk on the projection on the board. Joshua and Esteban are explaining what confuses them and she is trying to isolate the properties she wants them to attend to. She shows how you can set the protractor at an angle on the paper [so its base is on one of the rays]. She has a transparent protractor she can lay it on the overhead and project onto the chalk board. Attention is *good*—I see no one off task from where I am.

The success of this activity depends on student focus on the teacher and on the sequence of the presentation, as well as on student involvement in estimating, asking questions, and demonstrating correct answers. Ms. Anderson asked for these things and got them. Unlike the situation in Ms. Corvo's room, there was no ritualized, often-repeated basis for this cooperation. It seemed likely to me that the constantly varying modes of presentation and activity in Ms. Anderson's room actually contributed to maintaining student attention; in fact, students were far less likely to be off task, even during teacher-centered activities, than they were in Ms. Corvo's room. Even when Ms. Anderson assigned an activity like the following, for which she gave directions that allowed few student choices of how to respond, nearly all the students were fully involved.

> Sue Anderson: Get out a sheet of loose-leaf paper—fold it in half the long way. At the top of one side, write *advantages* and on the other side, write *disadvantages*. Now take 5 minutes within your group to list the advantages and disadvantages of exploring in space.

* * *

Reading this chapter might give the impression that these strategies of contributing to the construction of power relations by making decisions when students are not present always went unopposed in the three classrooms I observed. This was far from the truth. Students had a wide repertoire of their own contributions to building the structure called "What Teachers and Students Can Do Here." Students forced teachers' concealed strategies into the open, and located the seams into which they could insert their own efforts to promote their agenda of freedom from adult control. These actions are described, along with other student contributions to classroom power relations, in chapter 8.

Chapter 6

"Sally, Would You Like To Sit Down?" How Teachers Use Politeness and Indirect Discourse

ℰℴ ◆ ℭℬ

"Sally, would you like to sit down?" If Sally is a visitor in my home or office, I might ask this as a genuine question, or at least a suggestion. Sally might answer that she'd rather stand and admire the view from the window, or that she'd been sitting for hours in the car and would prefer to stay on her feet for a while.

But suppose that Sally is a student, and I am a teacher, and I say, "Sally, would you like to sit down?" The most likely interpretation of what I have said is a direct command, "Sit down, Sally." The most likely result is that Sally will take a seat.

White (1989) pointed out that "unrelenting politeness" is an "institutionalized presence" in American public schools. Yet, as he said, everyone recognizes what lies behind the politeness—the institutionalized authority of teachers. Rare is the classroom where teachers and students have built power relationships in which a student need not attend to a command or request from a teacher (see Swidler, 1979, for descriptions of free schools where such rare classrooms existed). So what is going on when teachers who mean "Sit down," say "Would you like to sit down?" or "Please, will you sit down," or even, "I would like to get started"—yet children respond to what seem to be polite requests or neutral statements as though they were in fact commands? Why do my observations from three elementary classrooms in three different schools contain so many instances of teachers' contributing to the construction of power relations, not in overt or obviously authoritarian ways, but in ways that seem to soften the edges of their claims to control student actions? Why do teachers make such heavy use of politeness formulas and indirect discourse strategies as they further the colluded-on agenda of cooperation in learning?

The question of when, how, and why speakers use language in ways that do not convey lexical meaning has been a focus of sociolinguistic study. Its examination has taken place in the following sequence: Searle (1966) developed the concept of *indirect speech acts*, which may have an apparent meaning quite different from their actual force in the conversation; Grice (1975) suggested that when someone makes a statement whose real meaning is different from its surface meaning, there is a reason, an intention, behind the discrepancy; and Brown and Levinson (1978) hypothesized that the principal reason for using politeness formulas is to avoid threatening the "face," or personal dignity, of other participants, and that they are used more often by weaker participants than by stronger.

In this chapter, I ask why teachers use these discourse strategies, and how they are related to the structure of power relationships that teachers and students build in classrooms, and to the agendas pursued by teachers and students.

INDIRECT DISCOURSE STRATEGIES

The term *discourse strategies* as used here is derived from Mishler's (1972) discussion of the effects on classroom relationships and learning of teachers' decisions about how to speak to students. He used the term to refer to a variety of choices a teacher might make about what to say and how to say it, and to the patterns of such choices that become apparent. He spoke of both direct and indirect discourse strategies chosen by teachers; interestingly, his analysis indicated that indirect strategies were a mark of superior teaching.

Delpit (1988) and others have suggested that this is a culturally based assumption that leads to miscommunication, adopting the widespread belief that use of such formulas and strategies is a characteristic of White American culture, and that students of color do not understand that they are being told what to do when a teacher uses them. These writers suggest that in the homes of children from various minority groups, adults address children very directly, and that nonminority teachers confuse them when they use indirect discourse to express their wishes.

McDermott and Roth (1978), however, held that people placed in cross-cultural groups quickly learn to understand what others are communicating, or to comprehend the expectations of others, as they jointly construct a context for interaction. When "communication problems" persist, they have another source besides misunderstanding. Specifically, they described an incident in which a classroom power relationship was being constructed. They found a child violating three established norms of his classroom (he touched the teacher on the buttock, called her by her last name without a prefix, and interrupted her as she worked with a small group), norms that, at other times, the child revealed he knew. As a result of these actions, he succeeded in getting the teacher to scold another student with whom he had been arguing. It is in the detailed analysis of the three unusual actions of the boy that McDermott and Roth found the interactions that create and construct the context, the social order. Seeing the success of the boy's actions in attaining his goal, they rejected the idea that his "inappropriate" actions came from culturally based ignorance of classroom norms; he had in fact used them very skillfully.

Whether or not it is true that the use of politeness formulas and indirect discourse strategies are associated with good or effective teaching, each of the teachers I observed used both direct and indirect strategies, though in varying proportions.

Teachers choose discourse strategies of indirection when, instead of stating or telling directly what they want, they speak to their students in a more oblique way. These strategies included the following:

- Using politeness formulas (these forms of speech are discussed in more detail below).
- Using speech acts whose surface meaning was not the same as their meaning in the interaction.
- Placing themselves with the class, rather than underlining their status as teacher (one way of doing this was using the pronoun *we*, rather than *you* or I; Brown & Levinson [1978] named this as a face-saving strategy).
- Praising desired behavior rather than criticizing undesired behavior.
- Stating general principles of behavior, rather than scolding or giving commands.
- Asking for student opinions about process decisions.
- Correcting student behavior unobtrusively, by a touch or silent gesture, rather than by giving a command.
- Offering many choices to students (but always from a range of possibilities that they themselves had selected and approved).

Two of these strategies were used by all the teachers during my observations; they were politeness formulas and speech acts whose surface meaning was not the same as their meaning in the interaction. These strategies are described generally, with examples from all the teachers. The use of the other strategies differed among the four teachers (three classroom teachers and the student teacher), so they are discussed in the individual contexts where they appeared.

Politeness Formulas

Politeness formulas used by the teachers included:

- Questions in place of commands: "Sally, would you like to sit down?" in place of "Sit down, Sally."
- Mentions in place of commands: "Sally, your desk is messy," in place of "Sally, clean up your desk."
- Statements of preference in place of commands: "It's really better if desks are tidy," in place of "Clean up your desks."
- Requests that use *please, thank you, excuse me,* and similar words, or are expressed conditionally (using modals like *would* or *could*) in place of commands: "Please sit down," or "Could you sit down?" in place of "Sit down."

The teachers I observed consistently used these polite forms in their speech to students, much more often than they gave direct commands. Yet, they seemed to expect that students would comply with polite requests without question, and were surprised or displeased if they did not do so.

Here are some examples of teachers using politeness formulas. They are taken from field notes and videotapes:

In a group discussion time, one of Ms. Kaminski's students was speaking, but a number of other students were chattering.

Ms. Kaminski: Please do him the favor of listening to him. [meaning: be quiet]

Ms. Anderson: All right, boys and girls, will you open up your assignment notebook? [meaning, open your notebook].

The children are seated in a circle on the rug. Ms. Kaminski is showing them an ABC book. The page they are looking at has the word BARN in large letters to represent the letter B. Someone says, "ABC." One of the students who can read, says loudly:

Nick: It's not BC. It's BA.
Ms. Kaminski: Nick, could you please use a gentle voice, because it's the main job of people in the first grade to try, and it's hard to try if people yell at you when you are trying.

Ms. Anderson: It's really better if I hear just one voice. [meaning, be quiet].

Indirect Speech Acts

In all three classrooms, I also saw teachers use speech acts whose surface meaning was not the same as their meaning in the interaction. A classic example of this occurs when two people are in a room: One says, "I'm cold," and the other rises and shuts the window. "I'm cold" can be interpreted as having meant, "Shut the window." Here are some examples of such speech acts; first, four ways of saying, "Be quiet:"

> Ms. Kaminski: I have two children who need to work on their listening. [meaning, you two be quiet].
> Ms. Corvo: I need your help. [meaning, be quiet].
> Ms. Anderson: I wonder if you can hear Patel—he's got some good ideas. [meaning, be quiet].
> Ms. Bridgestone: Excuse me. [meaning, be quiet].

When these strategies were used, it was not always completely clear to me, an outsider, whether choices were being offered to the students, or whether they had to comply regardless of how the teacher's wishes were expressed. My judgment on this question was based on the students' responses, believing that as regular participants in the power relations of their classroom, they were the experts on what the teacher "really meant" (McDermott & Roth, 1978). Two incidents from Ms. Kaminski's room illustrate how the students' responses clarified the teacher's meaning for me:

> Carlton is sitting directly in front of a child who is having a reading turn when the students are gathered on the rug.

> Ms. Kaminski: Carlton, why are you sitting in front of him? [meaning, move over, Carlton].

> Carlton moves over.

> Ms. Kaminski: Thank you very much. [Her thank you confirms that he has complied with her concealed command.]

> The students are gathered on the rug.

> Ms. Kaminski: Noah, you have something in your hand. Would you look at it and see what you need to do? [meaning, get rid of what you are holding].

> Noah looks at his hand, leaves the rug, and puts whatever it is in the trash. (Obviously, he has understood her meaning.)

I noticed considerable variation among the four teachers in their use of other kinds of indirect discourse strategies and in their willingness to use more direct strategies. Because of this variation, the next sections emphasize the particular strategies and choices of each teacher in turn. It was especially interesting that Aileen Corvo and Courtney Bridgestone, working with the same group of children, often on the same day, were quite different in their choices. In some cases, there was an opportunity for the teachers to give reasons for the variations in their practice that I observed. When these explanations were available, I have included them.

* * *

Sunny Kaminski, the teacher in the first-grade classroom, selected discourse strategies that covered a range from highly direct to extremely indirect. She quite consistently shifted between direct statements of expectations for students' actions and indirect statements about the learning activities they should engage in. She seemed to prefer making more direct contributions to classroom power relationships in the realm of student behavior and less direct ones in that of student learning.

Here are some of her direct statements concerning student behavior:

Ms. Kaminski: Carlton, sit on your bottom.

Ms. Kaminski: Erin, stay here. Don't get up.

Yet, sometimes there was room for indirection, or even negotiation, in interactions related to student behavior. As these examples imply, this was more common when interactions were close to the "border" between behavior and learning.

The students are gathered on the rug while Ms. Kaminski reads a story to them. When she finishes the story, she says:

Tell you what. If you would come over here and choose a book and then find someplace in the room to read it it would be just great.

On this morning, a monarch butterfly is emerging from its chrysalis in a terrarium. During readers' workshop, Carlton has become deeply involved in watching this process. When Ms. Kaminski calls the children to the rug, he is very unwilling to come. She calls him several times without response, and then says:

Ms. Kaminski: Give me five minutes with these kids and at snack time we'll look at it, I promise. And you can tell me what you saw.

Carlton comes reluctantly to the rug and sits down.

Ms. Kaminski often used the indirect discourse strategy of stating general principles of behavior rather than criticizing the behavior of a particular child. In the instance that follows, she could have tried to find out who had broken Charles' jet and punished that person. Instead, she waited until all the children were gathered and spoke to them generally about what had happened.

During cleanup, Charles discovers that someone has broken his jet [which he made earlier from plasticene]. He asks again and again:

Am I allowed to fix it?

Finally the aide says he can do it later, and he goes to sit on the rug, looking distressed. He has not helped clean up.

Once the children are gathered on the rug, Ms. Kaminski tells them that someone is unhappy because somebody messed up his work. She says that this really upsets people, and suggests what the children can do when they are finished cleaning up so they won't wander around breaking people's things.

The choice of this indirect discourse strategy had a number of benefits from Ms. Kaminski's point of view. She was able to bring Charles' problem to the other students' attention and show respect for his distress without developing the kind of adversarial situation between herself and the students that would contravene the colluded-on agenda of cooperation. Also, because Charles' distress was potentially disruptive to the cleanup process that she wants to support, she was able to avoid giving him strong encouragement for this behavior by making him the center of class attention. And she has avoided the potentially unsuccessful process of finding out who is responsible for a misdeed that neither she nor Charles saw happening.

Ms. Kaminski made many statements offering the students a choice with respect to their learning activities. In an interview, she said she encouraged students to negotiate with her to carry out their own choices. She told of a time three children approached her during reading workshop, when her stated expectation is that children will be involved in reading. These three children asked that they be allowed to write, pointing out that when they were writing they were reading the words that they wrote. She said she thought this was wonderful, and told them in a typical phrase to "go for it!"

The next instance illustrates well the cautious indirection with which she approached issues around the children's work. She wanted to offer the students choices, but she also had quite specific intentions for them. One day I heard her seeking a delicate balance between the two impulses:

It is time for writers' workshop, and Noah, Jane, Janet, and Pearl are working at one of the tables. At the moment, none of them is writing; all are drawing. One of the aims that Ms. Kaminski has at writers' workshop time [she said in interviews and in statements to the class] is to encourage these first-graders to actually begin to write, using invented spellings, and often captioning or commenting on drawings they have made. Ms. Kaminski comes up to the table and squats down next to Pearl.

Ms. Kaminski: What are you doing here? What's your topic?
Pearl: My friend.
Ms. Kaminski: Your friend. So you like to draw first when you write?
Pearl: Yes.
Ms. Kaminski: Do you ever write words with your drawing?

Ms. Kaminski's choice of the word *topic* here is part of an indirect discourse strategy through which she suggests that writing is a preferred activity. Children's drawings are not usually thought of as having topics; pieces of writing have topics. Similarly, the question, "So you like to draw first when you write?" has an indirect meaning; it implies that writing will take place, even if after drawing. Pearl could draw and not write at all, but that is not what Ms. Kaminski wants her to do. In the final sentence of the text, Ms. Kaminski uses a question ("Do you ever write words with your drawing?") rather than stating a rule, such as "We write words at writer's workshop time," or giving a command like, "Write, don't just draw."

* * *

Aileen Corvo, the supervising teacher in the fifth-grade classroom, used far fewer indirect discourse strategies with students than the other teachers. It is hard to be sure to what extent this contrast was a matter of style or philosophy, or was a more temporary result of the negative experience she said she had with her class of low-achieving students between September and March, when my observations began. Clearly, she was at this time far less committed than the other teachers to the colluded-on agenda of cooperation and courtesy.

Ms. Corvo used strategies that asserted her power directly, minimized student power, and separated her relationally from her students. She made little attempt to conceal her view of herself as the most powerful person in the classroom. For example:

Ms. Corvo goes to the front of the room and calls for attention.

Ms. Corvo: I don't have you with me and I can't function if I don't have you with me and I don't have control. I [she taps her chest audibly] must have control.

Ms. Corvo stands in the front of the room, ready to begin the lesson.

Ms. Corvo: Give me your attention. That's right, your undivided attention—only on me, the Golden Girl. [aside to Ms. Bridgestone, the student teacher:] I love that show. I need your attention and I'm not waiting much longer.

Ms. Corvo is telling the class what to do next.

Ms. Corvo: Peter, none of you are talking while I am. Peter, I am an important person.

Ms. Corvo used pronouns designating her own separateness from the group of students, as well as asserting her ownership of classroom supplies and naming the purpose of an activity as "providing her with information about what students know" (rather than, perhaps, "giving students opportunities to learn").

Ms. Corvo: If *you* play with *my* rulers I'll have to take them from you.

Ms. Corvo is introducing a lesson in which the class is to make "story frames" concerning the novel they are reading. This is an activity they have done before for other novels.

Ms. Corvo: What skills do the story frames show me you have?

She used vigorous control statements and even threats to assert her own position of power:

A student returns from the bathroom and replaces the large wooden key which serves as a bathroom pass on its hook. Lewis stands up while Ms. Corvo is at the front of the room talking and picks up the key, apparently heading for the bathroom.

Ms. Corvo: (sounding furious) Excuse me sir, how dare you? I am teaching a lesson. You know my rule.

She takes the key from Lewis and bangs it down on the table next to her.

Ms. Corvo has opened the morning with a lecture on proper behavior in the halls. Students, she says, are not to yell back and forth or speak rudely to teachers.

Ms. Corvo: You know I'm crazy enough so you don't try it with me. Just try loudcapping me and you'll hear Mean Joe Greene. Don't try it with me. [Later, she said in an interview that the reason for the lecture was that Donald, one of the students in the class, was rude to her in the hall on the previous day.]

Yet, there are still instances in my observations of Ms. Corvo using politeness formulas and indirect discourse strategies. Even for her, the colluded-on agenda was still in place at times:

Ms. Corvo: Let's not call out.

Some of the students are talking.

Ms. Corvo: No one is talking. [meaning, be quiet].

* * *

Courtney Bridgestone used a number of indirect discourse strategies as she worked with the children. Her personal style in the classroom was quiet, cool, almost self-effacing, and the colluded-on agenda seemed natural to her. She typically placed herself *with* the class through the discourse strategies she employed; she used indirect statements in asserting control over the class; her speech suggested that she and the class were working together, and that the class had important contributions to make to that work. For example, she often chose to use the pronoun *we* in place of *I* or *you*:

The class is in the midst of a discussion and has gotten quite noisy.

Ms. Bridgestone: I can't hear you when you all speak at once. OK, let's not call out so we can hear each person.

She openly took the students' opinions into consideration when making process decisions:

They are doing the practice tests for the Iowa Test of Basic Skills.

Student: Can we go ahead to do the rest of the problems?
Ms. Bridgestone: Hmmm, yes, do the whole page. That makes sense to me.

Ms. Bridgestone chose a number of other strategies that placed her with the group. For instance, she used humor quite frequently, laughing with the students at the jokes she made:

In reading the novel [*The Cybil War*], they have come to a part in which the fifth graders in the story find a magazine on an older sisters' bed. The magazine is open to a "love test," which they decide to take.

Ms. Bridgestone: Now listen to this, guys. You can find out if you're in lo-o-ove.

Students and teacher laugh together.

She sometimes called for a reading turn as if she were one of the students:

Ms. Bridgestone: Let me read a minute [...], let me read.

On occasion she asked for their help and even expressed admiration for their possession of skills she did not have:

Darin has made a cover for a story he has written and has lettered the title using glitter and glue. He has done a very neat job. Ms. Bridgestone praises him:

Ms. Bridgestone: I could never have done it that well. I have trouble with the glue.

Ms. Bridgestone sometimes defined assignments in terms of what the students would gain from them, rather than simply stating that they had to be done. For example, she told them that the purpose of one assignment they were doing was to help develop their self-confidence as they read by proving to them that they were able to figure out the meaning of words from their context.

When she stated a rule, it was often as a class norm or general principle, rather than as a command of her own:

At the end of one day's reading, Ms. Bridgestone passes out slips of paper on which each student is to write a sentence of 25 words or less to add to the "Simon Newton Sad, Sad Sentences Collection" [mentioned in the novel they are reading]. The response to this is fairly silly and Ms. Bridgestone has trouble keeping a straight face about it herself. When the students start reading their sentences aloud, the first sad sentence read is, "I came to school and I saw Marlon" [a student in the class]. The students find this extremely funny. Ms. Bridgestone scolds them in these terms:

Ms. Bridgestone: That kind of thing is not appreciated in this room and laughing when someone says something mean is not appreciated either.

Ms. Bridgestone also had other strategies for promoting the public agenda of cooperation by controlling children's behavior silently and unobtrusively, while allowing the flow of classroom interchange to continue uninterrupted. Sometimes she simply moved to stand next to an offending student, or touched a student lightly on the head or shoulders as a reminder to be quiet or to turn around:

Marlon is wiggling and is half out of his seat. He sits in the front row, so Ms. Bridgestone can simply reach down and touch his shoulder without moving from her place. He sits all the way down in his seat at her touch.

Except for one doubtful instance that is described in chapter 8, I never saw a class member who seemed to be confused by her indirect discourse strategies. It would be easy to think that using direct discourse strategies is simply better, more effective communication than using indirection; direct strategies might reduce confusion. However, the lack of evidence to support that idea—and the frequent use of indirection in ordinary communication—suggests that people are accustomed to using and understanding such speech acts. In fact, it would seem that in their use and acceptance of these patterns, students and teacher were colluding on the agenda of cooperation and courtesy.

* * *

About 2 years before I began to observe her classroom, Sue Anderson had made a conscious decision to do what she called "turn over some of the control of her classroom to her students." She consistently used this phrase to describe what she was doing, and reflected on the personal benefits she was reaping from the decision.

Many of the mechanisms for this transfer of control had become a routine part of life in her classroom. One was her use of what she called "positive language," which in most cases seemed to mean what I have called indirect discourse strategies, although it also included replacing direct criticism of students and their work with "finding something positive to say." In addition to frequent use of the politeness formulas and indirect statements previously discussed, she often told the students how she was feeling about what was going on in the classroom, wanting them to respond to her statement either by continuing their desirable behavior or by changing their undesirable behavior:

When Vincent starts to read there is a buzz of talk going on in the circle of children.

Ms. Anderson: Excuse me, Vincent, may I interrupt?

She turns to William and Kevin, who were among those talking.

Ms. Anderson: Boys, it's really hard for me to listen over here (she gestures toward Vincent) when there's noise over there.

The noise stops.

Like Ms. Bridgestone, she used the pronoun we to place herself with the class, rather than in opposition to it:

Ms. Anderson: What we need is one hundred per cent attention up here.

Because she had explicitly stated to the students her goal of sharing control of the classroom, Ms. Anderson made statements in the classroom about this sharing process:

Ms. Anderson: I don't know who to pick [for the next turn], so I'll turn the responsibility over to Damon .... Damon, anyone whose hand is up.

Nevertheless, this was a classroom where the majority of decisions about what learning activities to do when and how to do them were in the hands of the teacher. It was quite different from Ms. Kaminski's classroom, where the teacher believed that choosing what to do enhanced children's learning, and where a workshop atmosphere was encouraged. Unlike Ms. Kaminski, who was more likely to use direct statements with respect to behavior and indirect statements with respect to learning, Ms. Anderson was more often direct about learning than about behavior. Here, she is giving an assignment:

Ms. Anderson: Now, I want you to get out your notes from watching the video and make a list. Write down at least twelve birds or animals that we might see when we visit the marsh next week.

There's nothing indirect about that.

* * *

Some common threads stand out in what has already been said about teachers' use of indirect discourse strategies.

Every teacher used indirect discourse strategies and politeness formulas. There were many areas of differences among these teachers: their personal styles; their beliefs about whether, when, and to what extent students should have choices in the classroom; the degree of their commitment to the public agenda of cooperation; the frequency and contexts of their use of the indirect and direct strategies. Yet, each one did include indirect strategies and politeness formulas in her repertoire during the observations. I might even say that in all the classrooms I have visited in the course of my work, this is a universal. I haven't yet seen a teacher who is always direct.

There was little or no indication that the use of indirect discourse strategies was confusing to children. The idea that children were colluding with teachers in this agenda of cooperation was supported by the observation that children, regardless of their ethnicity, most often correctly interpreted the indirect strategies their teachers used, and responded to them as the teacher seemed to wish. This observation reinforces McDermott and Roth's (1978) contention that miscommunication is not a problem in classrooms—even cross-cultural classrooms, while countering the con- tention of Delpit (1988) and others that politeness formulas and indirect discourse strategies serve to confuse children who are not from the majority White culture.

Indirect discourse strategies were often used when the choice of response they implied was not intended to be, or could not possibly be, offered to the students. A clear example of such a situation in Ms. Kaminski's classroom follows:

The children are gathered on the rug for a sharing time; each has brought a book read during the preceding readers' workshop.

Ms. Kaminski: Oh-oh, the gym teacher will be here soon.

[From her tone and facial expression, I conclude that she has just realized that there is not enough time for very many children to share an entire book.]

Ms. Kaminski: Tell you what—why don't you just find your favorite page in your book? [meaning, you can only share one page of your book].

Clearly the constraints of time preclude Ms. Kaminski from actually offering the choice of letting each child share his or her entire book. If they should treat her indirect command as open to question, rather than as being polite, she would have to refuse their choice.

The kinds of situation in which indirect discourse strategies were used varied among the teachers. For two of them, Ms. Kaminski and to some extent Ms. Bridgestone, it was possible to see that indirect discourse strategies were more likely to be chosen in the area of children's learning activities, as opposed to the area of their behavior. Each of these teachers was more likely to use a direct statement or command to control children's behavior; indirect strategies appeared more often in the area of choices about learning. Ms. Corvo, who rarely used indirect discourse strategy, seemed not to favor them in either area. Ms. Anderson used such strategies more often in the area of behavior and less often in that of learning. It seems likely that this reflects each teacher's beliefs about teaching and learning. Ms. Kaminski stated clearly (in interviews) that she thought children learn best when they have choices about what to learn, so she tried to use discourse strategies that would not seem to impinge on the children's ability to choose. Ms. Anderson, on the other hand, believed that children should be able to choose more freely in the area of interpersonal actions, although she said (in an interview) that she was "not ready" to turn over to them many choices about what to learn.

There was an element of concealment in the use of the indirect strategies. Although students were offered, or appeared to be offered, choices, the teacher was fully in control of the range of choices available. This was most true for Ms. Kaminski, who believed that having choices would lead to more learning for the children. She stated strongly in interviews that she felt intensely responsible for students' learning and that her moves in this area were more carefully planned than those in the area of student behavior. She remarked that she regularly offered choices to students in the area of learning, but it was obvious that these were always choices between actions that were desirable from her point of view, and she said she believed that students learn better when they have the opportunity to choose.

Children did sometimes refuse to accept the polite or indirect discourse that was being offered to them and instead required the teacher to make a more direct statement. In this way, they forced the teacher's agenda to the surface so they could oppose it and prevented the teacher from maintaining the pretense that what was going on was cooperation and mutual politeness. Actions of this type are discussed in chapter 8.

* * *

Up to this point, I have tried to lay out what I saw, and what sense I made of it, but the questions I raised at the beginning of this chapter remain elusive. Why is it that teachers use indirect discourse strategies? Why do teachers choose to hide their agenda for children's learning behind the public agenda of cooperation and politeness? Why do teachers, who are supported in their contributions to building classroom power relationships by many of the institutional regularities of the school, seek to soften the edges of that power? Why do teachers make such heavy use of politeness formulas and discourse strategies as they further the colluded-on agenda of cooperation in learning?

According to Brown and Levinson (1978), politeness formulas are used to protect the "face," or public self-respect, of the listener. If the speaker is in a position of authority over the listener, saying "please" or using the conditional makes it less obvious that a command is being given to a person who is required to obey. Inversely, if the speaker is subordinate to the listener, using politeness conceals the fact that the speaker is telling the superior what to do.

This understanding of teachers' motivations is echoed by White (1989), who said:

> Thus, persons higher in status often treat persons lower in status with deference to ease the constraints of their inequity and to encourage a more free-flowing interaction and exchange of ideas .... [The teacher] uses deference to reduce the social difference between her and her pupils. (p. 303)

Such an analysis could suggest that teachers use politeness formulas because of their desire to protect the self-esteem of their students. These formulas allow them to avoid a continual emphasis on the strong contribution to the development of power relations that they make as teachers, adults, and possessors of greater knowledge. They might do this either because they wanted to preserve that self-esteem or because they wisely did not want to subdue students' thinking or provoke them to the point of rebellion.

A more subtle version of this analysis, as outlined by Cazden (1988), suggests that teachers do not feel so superior to their students, but in fact live in fear of an outbreak of student opposition, and use politeness formulas to steer clear of confrontations that they fear they may lose. Cazden recounted an incident in which she approached a student very cautiously, much concerned about his possible loss of face, but discovered with surprise that he was ready to be far more compliant than she expected.

Similarly, Courtney Bridgestone (a heavy user of indirect discourse strategies) discussed in an interview her concern that the children in Ms. Corvo's classroom, who reminded her of the ones who had bullied her when she had attended the very same school as a junior high school student, would refuse to obey her. She described how careful she tried to be to avoid provoking such incidents and to handle them well on the few occasions when they occurred.

This analysis could also reflect, not the fearfulness of teachers, but their sense that time wasted on putting down student rebellion is time lost from learning. Thus, the motivation for the use of indirect discourse strategies could circle back to the teachers' agenda of controlling student behavior in the interest of student learning. Sunny Kaminski and Sue Anderson talked about their belief that children do best when they have choices. I understood them to mean that the process of choosing was itself educational, that students show increased commitment to learning activities they have chosen themselves, and that they learn even from their errors, or "approximations," as Ms. Kaminski liked to call them.

Yet, a parallel interpretation could be that student choice is more efficient than teacher imposition—efficient in producing student learning. An alternative analysis could show that time on-task and seriousness of effort were increased by such teacher behaviors as offering choices and using indirect discourse strategies.

If this analysis were adopted, then the public agenda of cooperation and politeness (McDermott & Tylbor, 1986) that I have hypothesized would disappear, revealed as only a manifestation of the teacher's own agenda of maximum student learning. And students could quite simply be seen as either collaborating with the teacher's agenda, possibly because they had discovered that commitment to learning was one way to have "an interesting day," (Fraatz, 1987, p. 31) or, at other times, promoting their own agenda of freedom from adult control.

My sense is that this last analysis is oversimplified, reducing complex classroom interactions beyond their lowest terms. Even the most reflective teachers, like Ms. Kaminski and Ms. Anderson, are not planning the smallest details of their daily actions to lead to a single, unified goal. Yet the point remains, the same point made by Mishler (1972), that indirect discourse strategies may be a sign of good teaching.

Chapter 7

Defining Classroom Knowledge:
The Part That Students Play

৪০   ◆   ଔ

Because schools are intended to be places where learning occurs, the question of what will count as knowledge is especially important. What counts as knowledge is a determining factor in what students actually learn. That is why this aspect of classroom power relationships—how students contribute to the process of determining what will count as classroom knowledge—is the focus of this chapter.

In traditional sociological and political analysis, the power to define what will count as knowledge is assigned to the teacher. The larger society—defined as the structure of the school, the expectations of administrators, parents, and community members, and all kinds of curriculum materials—is thought to influence the teacher's use of this defining power.

Although the actions of students described in this chapter are surely affected by the same larger society that influences teachers' actions, the analysis I present here focuses on student actions exerting influence on what will be learned in a given classroom. I stress this point because so many writers in education have focused on the influence of the teacher, or of society through the teacher. Some view this influence as a primary instrument for the oppression or control of students, particularly those who are culturally different from the majority; others see it as a necessary part of the transmission of the desirable aspects of an historic culture. Without denying that one of the ways teachers contribute to constructing classroom power relationships is to influence the definition of classroom knowledge, I look in this chapter at how students also influence this definition. In doing so I am opening up the possibility of looking at how the influence of the surrounding society works through the students, rather than only through the teacher.

Yet, I am not trying to answer questions about why, or under the influence of what outside forces, students promote certain knowledge and demote other knowledge. A primarily observational study like this one cannot seek out the reasons, affective or cognitive, for actions observed. Instead, I offer instances of teachers' and students' actions that appear to promote contrasting or cooperative agendas with respect to classroom knowledge—I have avoided speculating on the reasons for their choices.

Some researchers have observed students sharing in the process of defining classroom knowledge. For example, Alison Jones (1981), a researcher in New Zealand, described and named an instance of student control over what counts as classroom knowledge. She studied a classroom in which teachers tried to focus instruction on higher level thinking about their subject; they knew that such thinking would be necessary if the students were to pass school-leaving examinations. Students in the classroom resisted including in the curriculum anything other than facts that could be memorized; thus they effectively defined what would count for them as classroom knowledge.

A student Jones (1981) observed said, "Well, that's what we're really doing here, isn't it, the notes ... to get the notes" (p. 23). One girl said of the teacher, "She asks me to ask questions. I never ask questions. I just keep quiet and I always say, 'What?' when she asks me questions so she has to ask them twice" (p. 24). Another said, "We never talk if she, you know, wants us to say things ... talk about something. Everyone shuts up .... What's the point? It's a waste of time" (p. 24). Jones could only speculate about the roots of the student beliefs leading to this particular (and, as it happened, destructive to the students' chances of academic success) definition of classroom knowledge, but she showed clearly that these older students were well aware that they shaped what the teacher did.

Harry Wolcott (1987) similarly recounted his struggle, as teacher in a one-room school in a Kwakiutl village, to resist student definitions of what would count as classroom knowledge. He wrote:

> My pupils ... held very rigid expectations about the activities they considered appropriate for school work. Insistence on attention to the three R's constituted the only legitimate kind of demand which the pupils both expected and accepted on the part of their teacher. ... the pupils responded most favorably to ... the specific tasks required in arithmetic and spelling. ... My attempts to relate social studies to their own lives made them uncomfortable both because they perceived this as prying and because I did not depend on textbooks in my approach. (p. 140)

In a related vein, Michelle Fine (1991), who studied the politics of dropouts in New York City, gave a vignette of a high school student constructing her own definition of classroom knowledge. She told how a social studies teacher set up an in-class debate on Bernard Goetz, the so-called "subway vigilante." The teacher told those who agreed with Goetz to go to one side of the room and those who disagreed to go to the other. This command defined the question of violence and responses to it as having only two possible answers. A number of students stayed in the middle of the room, and the teacher scolded them: "Don't be lazy. You have to make a decision. Like at work. You can't be passive .... Those of you who have no opinions, who haven't even thought about the issue, you won't get a chance to talk unless we have time" (p. 42). According to Fine:

> Deidre, a Black senior, bright and always quick to raise contradictions otherwise obscured, advocated the legitimacy of the middle group. 'It's not that I have no opinion. I don't like Goetz shooting up people who look like my brother, but I don't like feeling unsafe in the projects or in my neighborhood either. I got lots of opinions. I ain't bein' quiet 'cause I can't decide if he's right or wrong. I'm talkin'. (pp. 42–43)

Deidre actively expanded the teacher's dichotomous notion of "having an opinion" to one that took account of shading and context. She influenced, at least for herself and perhaps for others in the class, what would count as classroom knowledge.

The students in Jones' and Fine's studies are older than the ones I observed; they are more explicit about their part in defining classroom knowledge than were the first and fifth graders in my study. Yet, I frequently observed these young students engaged in the same process.

MS. CORVO'S ROOM:
DEFINING THE RANGE OF KNOWLEDGE

One way of defining what will count as knowledge is to decide what range of knowledge will be open for consideration at any one time. This question underlies the distinction between holistic and fragmented educational methods. For example, in teaching students to read, the teacher can focus broadly on the entire text, with all the meaning and aids to comprehension it offers, or on the details of the correspondence between spelling and sound. For the teacher, making this kind of decision about what will count as knowledge is like focusing a microscope lens. A wider and less precisely defined field can be chosen, or the focus can be tightened so that only a narrow segment of the field is in view. In the classrooms I studied, I saw teachers who had chosen a particular focus, but who found that focus modified by student actions.

Aileen Corvo's fifth-grade classroom, where the teachers generally tried to control all areas of student action, proved to be a rich source of such examples of student refocusing of the lens defining what would count as classroom knowledge. During one spelling test, I saw LaToya widen the teacher's focus for herself two times. This class had a weekly spelling pretest on Wednesday and the test on Friday, conducted according to rigid patterns of expected behavior. There seemed to be little room for student influence on what was occurring, and LaToya's actions were subtle though revealing:

It is so quiet. All the students are writing, focused on their papers. Ms. Bridgestone pronounces word number 5, period. There is a giggle from LaToya, who appears to be entering puberty.

Ms. Bridgestone pronounces the next word, *poet.* LaToya turns in her seat and looks at the text of "Stopping by the Woods on a Snowy Evening," which is posted on the wall.

In both these instances, LaToya's action did something that let the observer know, or at least make a strong guess, about what was in her mind as she heard the words on the spelling list. The words were part of a context of knowledge for LaToya; the teacher, through the spelling test activity, defined them only as collections of letters to be placed in the correct order. In this class, spelling lists were sharply marked as worthwhile knowledge, and because they came from books prepared outside the class, they had only the most tenuous connection with the students' actual use of words in reading, speaking, and writing. LaToya refused to leave the spelling words in this disconnected state; she redefined what would count as knowledge for her in that moment.

In contrast to this detached treatment of spelling and vocabulary, at another time Ms. Bridgestone (the student teacher) taught two lessons that were meant to build students' confidence in their ability to understand unfamiliar words with the help of context. She gave students a list of words from the novel they were reading. First, she asked them to guess what the words meant, using the context only; then she asked someone to look up the meaning of each word in a dictionary to confirm that the students' guesses were correct.

Here too, however, students were in conflict with her over what was to count as knowledge. She repeatedly affirmed that the students' sense of what the word meant, derived from the context, was valid knowledge. That was, in fact, the point of the lesson.

Keiyon and Donald, however, were both seen surreptitiously looking up the word meanings in their dictionaries and offering the dictionary definitions as meanings they had derived from context. They seemed to interpret the activity as a contest between the students and the dictionary, which they could win by cheating; they did not accept their guesses as valid knowledge. So they did not learn what Ms. Bridgestone intended to teach them: confidence in their own ability to use context as they read.

Another group of observations of Aileen Corvo's class contrasted the teachers' understanding with the students' understanding of what knowledge was supposed to be acquired through the writing workshop. The teachers thought of this as a time to learn to write well. If students followed the steps in the writing process (the teachers believed and told both students and interviewer), good writing would be produced, and the students would internalize a process that produced good writing. The steps in the process were permanently displayed on wall posters around the room, and were often reviewed with the students, either briefly in the course of giving directions or in a full-scale lesson. Everything that happened during writers' workshop, from the teachers' viewpoints, was in the service of "learning to write well."

The steps of the writing process involved an alternation of talking ("conferencing") with another person, either teacher or fellow student, and writing on one's own, each time incorporating suggestions from the conference. Conferences were intended to help students develop and expand their ideas, include interesting detail, and write with correct spelling, grammar, and punctuation.

Carrying out the process required that the norms of silence and lack of movement, usually enforced in this classroom, be disregarded at this time. One or even two teachers could never provide each student with the multiple conferences needed in this system for the development of each piece of writing, so students needed to conference with their peers. To do this, they had to move around the room.

Also, an essential element of this model of the writing process was that students were free to write on topics of their choice and to write pieces of the length they felt was appropriate for their topic. Teachers could not, if they wished to obtain the results promised by the process, exercise control over the content of student writing.

It appeared that from the students' point of view, the writers' workshop was nothing more than an opportunity to write and talk about topics that interested them, and to conduct social interchange on those and other topics with their friends; they did not seem to define learning to write well as knowledge in this context. Possibly, this was a result of the emphasis on the steps of the writing process—rather than on understanding what good writing actually is—that characterized writing process instruction in this classroom.

Some of the conferences the students held followed the "correct" format, which had been taught and practiced in writing minilessons. In this format, the writer reads the piece aloud and the listener asks questions, such as, "What did you mean by ____?" or makes comments, such as, "I would like to know more about ____."

Most of the time, students chose to conference with their friends, and as I walked around the room at this time I could hear them using their "conferences" to discuss a variety of topics, especially television shows, movies, and comic books. There was little or no evidence that they perceived the workshop as an opportunity to improve their writing. Marie, in fact, almost explicitly denied that goal in this interchange:

Marie: I finished my piece.
Ms. Corvo: Have you conferenced on it?
Marie: Yeah, I made it shorter so I wouldn't have to type so much.

The question of what topics students should write about in the writing workshop was also a matter of conflict between student and teacher wishes. Most students had a strong preference for themes of horror, gang warfare, and violence:

Ms. Bridgestone is at the chalkboard, and students are calling out their ideas for pieces they might write.
Voices call: Gangs! Vampires! Murders! Gangs in Los Angeles!

The teachers told both the class and the interviewer that they were uncomfortable when these fifth graders wrote about these topics, but were unsure how to respond. The writers' workshop principle that students should write about what interests them was in conflict with the teachers' sense of what constituted appropriate subjects to address in school. Students continued to choose the questionable topics most frequently. Their concerns and interests prevailed over what the teachers thought was suitable.

For example, the students wrote "modern fairy tales," that were to be displayed for parents and then sent to the principal of the school, who was ill. Many of them chose tales like Little Red Riding Hood and Three Billy Goats Gruff, stories that already contained elements of violence. They multiplied as well as modernized the level of violence in the tales. Many of them seemed more proud of and pleased with this work than with any other piece of school work I saw them do. Perhaps this was because they had succeeded in controlling what would count as classroom knowledge.

MS. KAMINSKI'S ROOM: CONFLICT OVER
WHAT COUNTS AS CLASSROOM KNOWLEDGE

In Ms. Kaminski's first-grade classroom, what Ms. Kaminski named as knowledge was most often accepted as such. She planned and prepared for her class rigorously, and the definition of knowledge that came out of this planning—an instance of her "invisible" contribution to building the classroom power structure—was usually the one that prevailed. Compared to traditional first-grade teachers, Ms. Kaminski used a broad focus in defining what would count as classroom knowledge, accepting much that would not everywhere be defined as proper first-grade knowledge.

For example, in this incident, Ms. Kaminski named an activity as part of the knowledge area "music," an official part of first-grade curriculum. This incident has to be understood against the possibility of her defining what the students did as "not music," or as some kind of inappropriate behavior:

The children are gathered on the rug and are singing with a tape which is playing on the stereo. Two of the boys go over to the table where the stereo is, pick up rhythm instruments, and join in with the song. When the song ends, Ms. Kaminski praises "the musicians."

Student: They're not musicians.
Ms. Kaminski: Musicians are people who make music. Weren't they making music with the bells and the tambourine? Then they're musicians.

During a math activity time, Ms. Kaminski shaped the students' work to match her definition of school knowledge. "Sorting" was considered, in this classroom, a proper part of school mathematics knowledge. Simply making judgments of "pretty" and "not pretty" was not. Ms. Kaminski introduced the word "sorting" into what the students were, in fact already doing:

Juana, Sara, and Jennifer were seated at one of the tables with a box of buttons. Each one had taken a handful of buttons and was looking at them, stopping to exclaim over and show to the others the particularly "pretty" ones. Ms. Kaminski came over and sat down with them. She picked up on their saying that they were finding the pretty ones and encouraged them to sort all the buttons into categories of "pretty" and "not-pretty."

Again, during readers' workshop, children were supposed to be involved with books. Reading, looking at a book, pretending to read, telling the story of a book while looking through it, listening to a tape while looking at the book it records, and reading with a friend or listening to a friend read were all defined as appropriate. Many other activities, such as painting, playing with blocks, or making patterns with Unifix cubes, were not to be done at this time. (At other times, they could be a source of classroom knowledge. Ms. Kaminski used the terms "working with blocks" and "working with Unifix cubes" to indicate that these activities were within the realm of classroom knowledge.)

During the first weeks of the year, however, the class was heavily involved in a study of insects, and Ms. Kaminski was willing to stretch the definitions for reading time to include this topic.

On the fifth day of school, most of the children were involved with books during readers' workshop. Nathaniel, however, was wandering around the room with the raccoon puppet, making it squeak. [This was an activity which clearly was not defined as relating to reading.] Ms. Kaminski suggested that he look at the monarch caterpillars. He did, and two other students joined him.

In this way, Ms. Kaminski defined "looking at caterpillars" as a source of school knowledge, and placed it on a par with "reading" as an appropriate activity during readers' workshop. In an interview, she said that as the year went on, students would be expected to read or write about animals and the like that they might be observing during readers' and writers' workshops, but that at this point, observing was enough.

All these instances illustrate how Ms. Kaminski worked to establish a definition of what would count as school knowledge in her classroom. Yet, at other times, even these young children were either welcomed by Ms. Kaminski to participate in defining what would count as knowledge in their classroom or created their own definitions of what knowledge would be brought into the classroom. For example:

> Thomas had used his free choice time to make a "map book," which he shared. He had put several cities in the United States on his maps. Ms. Kaminski pulled down a map of the United States, which hung next to her seat, and they pointed out various places on the large map. Someone asked where Africa is. Ms. Kaminski pulled down a world map. They looked at it and located places around the world for a few minutes.

Geography, as this might be called, may not be part of the planned first-grade curriculum, but it counted as school knowledge here, and Ms. Kaminski was ready to accept it.

> At other times, children were clearly creating these definitions against Ms. Kaminski's resistance. Certain children were highly successful in doing this; Andra, who was an African-American girl from a family living in poverty, was such a child. The children had Lincoln Logs to use during free choice time because it was before Thanksgiving and they were doing a unit on early Americans and because building with Lincoln Logs was defined by Ms. Kaminski as a math activity. [The logs are designed proportionally, so that notions of half, double and the like can be derived from working with them.] By this time in the year, "a math activity" was the one thing students must do during some part of free choice time. Andra had been asked to build a house with Lincoln Logs, but she had chosen instead to draw a house on paper, using Lincoln Logs as rulers to get straight lines. When she displayed the picture at sharing time, Ms. Kaminski told the children how Andra had made the drawing, but pointed out that tomorrow Andra *would* really use Lincoln Logs to build.

Andra's most powerful and successful effort to set up her own definition of classroom knowledge took place over many months. I first became aware of it when, at sharing time, Andra wanted to show a book into which she had copied words from *The Very Hungry Caterpillar*:

One of the children said that you were not supposed to copy words from books; you were supposed to write your own words. Ms. Kaminski said that was the rule during writers' workshop, but that Andra did this activity at free choice time, and it was OK if she used part of her free choice time to do that.

This interchange reflected Ms. Kaminski's belief that children learn to write by generating their own words through invented spelling, rather than by copying the words of others. Some children enjoyed copying from books or from others' writing, and she wanted to limit the time they spent on that, pushing them to what she saw as the more challenging task of "writing their own words."

Andra, however, persisted in copying words throughout the year when she was supposed to be reading or writing. It was one of her preferred activities, and she spent much time on this forbidden or marginally acceptable activity. By March, she had a large vocabulary of words that she could read and write, which she apparently had learned by copying. Along the way she had learned to sound out many words and to create invented spellings, but she preferred to learn words by copying them. She succeeded in at least partially substituting her own way of learning to read, her own definition of what constituted learning to read, for the one specified by Ms. Kaminski.

A somewhat related incident took place when Carlton chose to work at a table at which children were to write and draw pictures about the class guinea pigs, one of whom had given birth on the previous day. The aide was there to help them write about the guinea pigs. I had the impression that providing this rather defined activity was intended to help the children shift the focus of their interest in the guinea pigs because the mother and babies could not be safely touched soon after the birth. Yet, Carlton wanted to work with a book about monsters that he had brought from home:

Aide: No, this activity is about guinea pigs.

Carlton went to his cubby and got his book.

Aide: Put it back, Carlton.

Carlton complied, but stood looking carefully at the cover of the book before putting it in the cubby. Then he came back to the table and wrote MONST on his paper. He got up, went back to his cubby, pulled out the book and looked at it again. He returned to the table and wrote ERSW. Then he wrote KNEPK (an invented spelling of the words "guinea pig.")

Carlton: It says, "Monster Guinea Pig."

Then Carlton settled down to draw an elaborate picture of the cage with a guinea pig in it. There was nothing monstrous about the guinea pig he drew.

The last instance of conflict over what would count as classroom knowledge in Ms. Kaminski's classroom could be described as ideological. It took place during the study of insects, when there were monarch butterflies, their caterpillars and cocoons, and praying mantises in various terrariums in the room.

One morning, I happened to sit down next to a terrarium containing praying mantises. I noticed that two of them were mating. When Ms. Kaminski walked by, I pointed this out to her, as she was usually eager to share with the children anything new about the insects. She said that she and the aide had noticed what was happening, but were telling the children that the two mantises were very good friends and were playing together. Later, in an interview, I asked her about this event. She confirmed that she had decided not to include sexual reproduction in the study of insect life; she considered the topic inappropriate for first graders.

In connection with their insect study, the class had read Eric Carle's book *The Very Hungry Caterpillar*, and they were preparing a play based on it for parent night:

Ms. Kaminski was choosing volunteers for the various parts in the play, as they paged through the book from the beginning. Students had been chosen to play the caterpillar, the moon, and the various edibles that come into the story. There were several volunteers to be the butterfly, the last part to appear in the book. Ms. Kaminski chose James. Philip, Carlton, and another boy called out, "Who is the mate?" At first, Ms. Kaminski didn't understand what they were saying. They repeated their question and at last she did understand.

Ms. Kaminski: The story doesn't call for a mate. Does that answer your question?

The children's question seemed to represent exactly the kind of extension of ideas that Ms. Kaminski usually encouraged, but her response to it, like the first incident, put sexual knowledge firmly outside the category of classroom knowledge. Yet, even though she rejected it as part of the curriculum, the fact that several children raised it together indicates that it had in fact been part of the study for them. This incident is parallel to LaToya's giggle at the spelling word *period*. Teachers may strive to exclude sexuality from the definition of classroom knowledge; children may insist on including it.

SUE ANDERSON'S ROOM: INVITING
STUDENTS' LIVES INTO THE CURRICULUM

Of the three teachers, Sue Anderson was the one who most actively sought to engage children in defining classroom knowledge by bringing their own experiences and memories into their learning experiences. This was particularly true during language arts and social studies classes, when she often asked so-called "high-level questions" that called for connecting the subject at hand with other knowledge. Because her students were quite diverse, with about one fifth of the students she saw each day coming from families who had emigrated from at least five different countries, and close to the same number from American minorities, this shifting of the definition of classroom knowledge was often in a multicultural direction. Oyler (1996) made a distinction between cases when the students actually set the topic of discussion and those when the topic the teacher raises allows students to shape the content of the discussion out of their personal experience. Although the former is certainly a stronger instance of students contributing to classroom power relations, the latter exemplifies the sometimes collaborative nature of the development of those relations.

Ms. Anderson's willingness to allow students' home lives and interests to be defined as classroom knowledge was so great that she held a weekly "sharing time," at which children brought in objects they owned or had found or told stories about their lives outside of school. Because of this effort on her part, there was rarely an occasion when children redefined classroom knowledge against her will. Yet, it was their individual choices about what to share, what to bring, and what to say that contributed to defining what would be classroom knowledge.

In late fall, for example, the class was reading a popular children's novel called *Maniac Magee*. This novel deals with themes of interracial conflict and connection as it tells the story of the adventures of a homeless boy. Ms. Anderson had focused on the word *color-blind*, used in the book. She asked whether it was right to say that Maniac was "*color-blind*."

This turned out to be a hard question, because some students took it to refer literally to color-blindness, and they thought a color-blind person would see only black and white, like an old movie. And because the point in the book was supposed to be that Maniac did not notice any difference between Black and White people, the discussion got quite confusing. But it was an important idea in understanding the book. Maniac is strange in a number of ways, but his failure to understand this basic fact of American life, as the book presents it, is certainly part of the reason for his nickname.

Yuri, an Israeli boy whose family was temporarily living in the United States, offered a story to clarify the problem. He gave an example from Israeli history, of *sabras*, native-born Israelis, mistreating new immigrants. He pointed out that this was much the same thing that happened between

Whites and Blacks in the United States, but Maniac didn't understand this, and that was why he was called *color-blind*. Yuri, with his broader frame of reference, had shifted the focus of the discussion—and the definition of this bit of classroom knowledge—from racism in one small town, or in the United States, to conflict between groups in other places and for other reasons.

Some days later, while the class was still discussing *Maniac McGee*, Ms. Anderson brought up the matter of Maniac's homelessness and loneliness. "What could you do if someone you know seems lonely?" she asked. As at many other times, this question led several students to share information about their home situations with others in the class. Vincent, a member of a family that had immigrated from Vietnam, talked about his enjoyment of opportunities to be alone. At home, he said, he often had to take care of his younger siblings and got in trouble if they broke the rules. So he appreciated it when he could be on his own. In fact, that was why he would rather work alone in school, rather than in groups. Later in the year, when they were reading *My Brother Sam Is Dead*, Denny talked about how the tensions and disagreements in that family reminded him of feelings in his own home.

Another occasion of students' bringing in their home situations as school knowledge took place when they were reading *Sign of the Beaver*, a novel in which a White boy is asked to teach English to an American-Indian boy. Ms. Anderson was leading a discussion of how students would teach English to a speaker of another language, how the students who took French or Spanish before school were being taught, and how they thought they themselves would learn a new language best.

In this case, she directly solicited information from three of the students who were from immigrant families. Dara, from Iran, said that her family spoke Persian and that she sometimes did her homework in Persian and translated it into English. Avram, from Russia, said, "We speak Hebrew at home." Vincent said, "We speak Vietnamese. I mean, they speak it to me. I can understand it but I would never ever be able to say anything back to them." The three students opened up for the class a new sense of what knowing or learning a language could mean.

Later in the year, students made American Indian craft items as part of their study of Indian nations. Joshua was Oneida, and he used this opportunity to share with the class what he had learned from his mother, information about where you go to get clay and dyes to use in craft work. The authentic and elegant dream catcher he made also broadened the group's sense of what these crafts could be like—it was quite different from the crude pieces most of them produced.

One of the few instances I saw in Ms. Anderson's class in which a student shifted the definition of classroom knowledge away from the expected one without her participation and consent took place during math class. The students were in groups working on a problem-solving book; I observed a group that had settled on the floor next to the chalkboard. One of the problems was about going to a restaurant; it had several steps of making menu choices based on a budget and then figuring the bill. The directions said to figure a 15% tip. Esteban suggested that more than 15% was better, that they could pretend they were rich enough to give a bigger tip, and that waiters need bigger tips than that. They talked intensely about why and how much you tip until Kelly stood up, copied the method in the book onto the chalkboard, and said they should tip as much as the book said.

Clearly, the intention of the activity was to teach about solving math problems, not about restaurant behavior, but the group had redefined what would count as classroom knowledge and focused on an interpersonal rather than a mathematical issue.

In another math class, a similar event occurred. The class was working on a packet of word problems, of which the first was the kind where several people need to cross the river in a two-person canoe, but there are constraints on who can be left alone together on one or the other side of the river or in the canoe. One of the students suggested solving the problem by having two of the people swim across the river; again, this redefined the question from its problem-to-solve frame to a real-life context. The group refused to accept as classroom knowledge the constrained framework of a logic problem, and instead worked on a broader problem that could appear in their ordinary lives.

An instance of actual conflict in this area between Ms. Anderson and one of the students took place when Mark was working on his research paper. From Ms. Anderson's point of view, the classroom knowledge at issue was how to locate research materials in the library, how to take notes, how to combine material from different sources, how to plan a structure for the paper, and how to prepare a bibliography. The students had freely chosen their topics, and Mark had picked a favorite, Robin Hood. After several opportunities to take notes, Mark had two note cards, one listing the names of characters in the Robin Hood stories and one listing major incidents in the stories. It was becoming clear that his plan for the research paper was to tell the Robin Hood story from memory. This exchange took place:

Ms. Anderson: I think you need a better topic. A real research topic.
Mark: Naah. I like Robin Hood. I want to do it on Robin Hood.
Ms. Anderson: I think you're fighting me on this, Mark.
Mark: I just know a lot about Robin Hood in my head.
Ms. Anderson: That's not the point. This is a research paper.

Mark was trying to shift the activity to one focused on "writing what you know about a topic." Ms. Anderson insisted that it was about "doing research." This was clearly not something that Mark felt the need to learn. Ms. Anderson had to call Mark's parents and enlist their help before he agreed to produce an actual research paper.

* * *

I drew several conclusions from these observations of students and teachers defining what counts as classroom knowledge. First, the construction of a definition of what counts as classroom knowledge is an essential part of classroom power relations. It can be thought of as a substructure of the larger structure of permitted actions for teachers and students being built in the classroom. The name of this substructure is "What Students Can Learn Here." Students in each of the three classes could be seen engaging in this process, with or without the support of the teacher. As in other aspects of the development of power relations, teachers most often created a basic framework; students built areas—central or off to the side—in which they could operate independently. Sometimes they built them in ways that interfered with the framework the teacher had established.

Second, a number of the events that teachers saw as interfering with the framework they were constructing were connected with sexuality. Teachers seemed to prefer defining sexual knowledge as not suitable for the classroom. The culture of schools seeks to exclude students' sexuality, even making their denial of it a criterion for students' school success. Meanwhile, students seek to define this important part of their being as appropriate classroom knowledge. Such activity was observed by Grahame and Jardine (1990), who told how a teacher's question to a group of high school boys about the uses of fleece fabrics quickly led to a set of highly sexual and fanciful responses. The teacher ignored their comments completely, and said, "I'm just going to put linings [as a use for the fleece fabric]" (p. 295).

Third, the validity of the notion that schools, through teachers, reproduce culture and transmit culturally sanctioned knowledge depends on the premise that it is teachers who decide what will count as knowledge. This premise needs to be rethought in light of evidence that students are important contributors to such definition. An alternative explanation is that such reproduction and transmission are part of students' entire lives and are funneled *through the students*, as well as through the teacher, from the outside world into the classroom.

Last, teachers need to be aware of how students try to widen the focus of classroom knowledge from fragmented bits of curriculum to a more holistic vision of their world. They are constantly occupied with connecting and extending knowledge (Hynds, 1994). Consistently, students in the three classrooms (with or without their teachers' encouragement) were seen making connections between what was presented as classroom knowledge and what they knew from other experiences. Following Sue Anderson's lead by taking advantage of, rather than resisting, this process seems likely to result in stronger learning experiences for students.

Chapter 8

Students in Conflict
With Teachers' Agendas:
Interactive Contributions to
Classroom Power Relations

ೲ ◆ ೞ

This chapter takes a closer look at student participation in constructing classroom power relations. As they pursue their agenda of "having an interesting day," and collaborate in the shared agenda of cooperation in learning, as they build new rooms in otherwise unoccupied areas of the imaginary building that represents power relations in their classrooms, as on occasion they attempt to build a new room in an area occupied, or potentially occupied, by an existing or planned teacher-built structure, students, like teachers, are continually engaged in creating the "What Teachers and Students Can Do Here" structure.

Seeing and interpreting the actions of students has proved to be the most difficult part of this analysis. Equipped with tools from ethnomethodoloy, microethnography, sociolinguistics, and conversational analysis, I have tried to make rigorous yet imaginative interpretations of student actions.

Three barriers create the difficulty I experienced. First, the students are many, while the teachers are few. As an observational problem, recording and analyzing student actions is a much more complex task than recording and analyzing teacher actions. Inevitably, it is less complete.

Second, with the teachers, I am a peer. I could ask a teacher, often within moments, what she had been intending when a particular action took place. I could give teachers copies of transcripts, or show them videos of interaction in their classrooms, and engage in extensive discussion about their intentions and beliefs, correcting and developing my interpretations as I progressed. On-the-spot interviewing of students would be a serious intrusion in any classroom, and impossible in some. Though I know other researchers have done so, it seemed inappropriate to me to conduct extensive discussions, outside of class, with these young children. Certainly, it would have been difficult to negotiate such conversations with them, their teachers, and their parents, but I was also concerned that my questions might shape not just their answers, but their developing views of their teachers and of their own place in the classroom.

Third, although I am deeply convinced by my own experience as a classroom teacher and by many hours of observation and thought of the interactive constructivist nature of classroom power relations (as I have described them throughout this book), I have still been socialized—and still am under cultural pressure—to see teachers as playing a highly dominant role in those relations. To see students in particular situations as the influential construction workers I am certain they are, I must constantly push beyond my first responses to a deeper understanding of the actions I am observing. I found that a great support in this process is the related analysis of other observers, and this chapter has deep roots in the work of Courtney Cazden, Ray McDermott, Hugh Mehan, Alison Jones, Harry Wolcott, Celia Oyler, Michelle Fine, and others.

Because of the somewhat counterintuitive nature of the analysis in this chapter, I felt it was necessary to include large numbers of detailed and specific examples to support the points I am seeking to make.

STUDENTS ACTIONS THAT CONFLICT
WITH TEACHER AGENDAS

I found it easiest to see student contributions to classroom power relations when they were highlighted by being in direct conflict with the contributions of teachers. For that reason, these kinds of actions are the first discussed in this chapter.

Students Conflicting With Designed Activities to Limit Their Responses

In Aileen Corvo's classroom, where the day included many activities intended to offer students a limited choice of responses, there were many instances of student actions that conflicted with teacher-planned activities. Griffin and Mehan (1981) spoke of the "seams in the lesson discourse," cracks in the regular patterns of teacher-to-student-to-teacher talk, of which students learn to take advantage (p. 201). In a room like Ms. Corvo's, the requirements of many of the activities the teacher has planned are so explicit, and the "seams" into which the students can insert their own words and actions so few, that it might seem difficult for students to make their own contributions to power relations. Yet, I saw many small-scale actions by students as they picked at those seams. The disruptive effect of these actions depended in part on how many students were engaged in them at any one time; if the actions were very numerous, they might interfere seriously with the teacher's agenda.

For example, students could misunderstand what the teacher had said, or what she wanted them to do. (Cazden, 1988, in her book describing her year of teaching first grade, also identified this as one of the ways students contributed to power relationships in her classroom.) In Ms. Corvo's room, the students were taking a spelling test on a word list they had been studying for a week, including writing out the words 5 times each and 10 times if a word was missed on the pretest. It seems likely that they were familiar with the words, yet interactions like this were common:

> Donald: Is that idea or ideal?
> Ms. Bridgestone: Ideal.

A few minutes later:

> Donald: What?
> Ms. Bridgestone: Station.

At the beginning of another such spelling test:

> Marlon: What unit?
> Ms. Bridgestone: Stadium.
> Marlon: No, what unit?
> Ms. Bridgestone: Twenty-five.
> LaToya: You can see it on the board.

Even LaToya, another student, is surprised by Marlon's asking a question whose answer is clearly visible a few feet from his desk. In the meantime, the orderly progression of the spelling test, seemingly an impregnable regularity of the classroom routine, as described in chapter 5, has been delayed again and again by these "misunderstandings."

Similar actions occurred during the round-robin reading activity that was such a predictable part of the day's routine.

At the beginning of reading time:

> Ms. Bridgestone: Take out your *Cybil War*. We're on page 102.
> Voices: 98? What page? What page did you say we're on? Did we have this for homework?

Other actions by students that conflicted with structured activities include wiggling silently or pushing the limits of "sitting in a seat." Sometimes as many as half a dozen students of the 20 or so present in Ms. Corvo's room were wiggling or tapping. From my notes:

LaToya taps, wiggles, and sits crooked, half off her chair.
Andrew is twitching his leg, and June her foot.
June, Andrew, and James are all twitching.

Again, students can simply tune out, withdrawing their attention and their energy. This may mean a daydreaming kind of inattention, or covert involvement in some other activity. An occasional event in Ms. Kaminski's and Ms. Anderson's classrooms, this was a major theme in Ms. Corvo's:

It is oral reading time. One of the students is reading aloud. Lewis is in and out of the book. Sometimes he is in for ten seconds or out for twenty seconds. He taps the book on his knee. He hasn't turned a page for a long time. I suspect he does not know where they are in the book.
The three students who are most out of it are Rosie, Darin, and Lewis. Lewis is constantly shifting his attention in and out of the room, in and out of the book, inspecting his forearm, fooling with a rubber band. Darin seems spaced out, staring at the ceiling, or nearly asleep with his head on his desk. Rosie sits up, holds the book in front of her and has her eyes in that direction. She does a good imitation of someone who is on task. But she rarely turns a page or responds to the content of the book (sad or humorous) or to the discussion. Keiyon is filling in a workbook page which he is holding in his lap so that his desk hides what he is doing from the teacher.

Another action available to students is to call out comments on what is being said or done. This can be done either loudly enough for the entire class and the teacher to hear, or *sotto voce*:

Ms. Corvo is giving a spelling test. She reads each word, and then gives a sentence using the word. Each of the sentences is related to these students and this classroom. [Ms. Corvo: Produce. In writing workshop you like to produce nice work.] Someone calls out a response to one of the sentences.

Ms. Corvo: Let's not call out.

Ms. Corvo has asked the class for responses to a question about Sadako, the hero of the novel they are reading.

Paul: Sadako loves to run and believes in good luck charms.
Andrew: She runs like the wind.
Keiyon: [softly] She does not. The wind doesn't run.

A relatively radical action, one that many of the students never choose, is simply to get up and move. This is definitely unacceptable in Ms Corvo's room:

LaToya gets up during oral reading and goes to the trash can.

Ms. Bridgestone: Sit down, LaToya.

LaToya complies with obvious irritation.

Lewis gets up and goes to the pencil sharpener.

Ms. Bridgestone: No, Lewis, not now.

Lewis turns back to his seat with a disgusted look.

In Ms. Anderson's room, on the other hand, such an action is likely to be ignored:

Ms. Anderson starts a video.

Various students: Notes, notes, we have to take notes.

Shonda hunkers down behind a table.

Shonda: I'm hiding from the notes.

In a moment, she gets up and goes to her chair.

Ms. Anderson: This video is good, better than the one we saw last week. It's about exactly what we're doing.

On another day:

The class is working in small groups to answer questions. Then they report their results to the class as a whole. During this part of the discussion, Shonda, who was sitting with a group in the back of the room, sits in her chair as she scoots it around the room—about 20 feet—to her seat. All ignore this. (There is little noise, on the carpeted floor.)

In Ms. Anderson's room, as in Ms. Kaminski's, there were few activities that placed strict limits on how students could respond, and those that did occur were usually new to the students. This may be why there were few instances—and those were quite minor—of students engaging in actions that interfered with such activities. Ms. Anderson taught in a team situation. The five-paragraph essay was an extended activity that came from the team and was specifically designed to prepare the students for their middle school experience. It offered very limited response choices. In this situation, the kinds of actions that were commonplace in Ms. Corvo's room appeared in Ms. Anderson's:

> They are working on a five-paragraph essay. The topic is: Exploring [something]. They have picked what to explore [a country, a desert or mountain or ocean, a planet], and filled in an outline for the essay that has been given to them.
>
> Shonda doesn't seem to understand the concept of *outline* and is messing hers up. Jack starts to write a story and is angry when told it's great but not the assignment. For Michelle this is a huge writing assignment—it's hard for her to stay on task. They are used to setting their own structure and using their creativity when they are writing, and this is much more directed.
>
> At one point I see six children who are off task: Pat is drawing a picture, which Jack is trying to see. Shonda is whispering to Kelly (who is working). Joshua is staring out the window; Sarah is rearranging her pencil box. Denny is out of his seat and wandering around the room. These are children who are usually involved in whatever activity is going on—but not this one.

These kinds of actions are easy to notice because they are undoubtedly outside the teacher's expectations for the structured activities during which they take place, and because, especially when they occur often, they are clearly disruptive of the teachers' plans. When students are misunderstanding, wiggling, tuning out, calling out comments, and even getting up and moving around, especially during activities in which students are supposed to produce a specified response, everything takes longer and requires more effort from the teacher. In these situations, teachers are seen intervening to put a stop to them (see Morine-Dershimer, 1985, who indicated that even the most minimal need for such interventions interferes with the success of the teacher's agendas), and the teacher's agenda of promoting student learning is curtailed.

Student Rejection of the Teacher's Assumptions

In Ms. Corvo's room in particular, I saw students implicitly rejecting some quite basic assumptions that teachers were making about what would motivate students, or about what the teachers could effectively do to promote their agenda of controlling student actions for the purpose of student learning. Such rejections are particularly difficult for teachers to deal with because they counter assumptions that are often unexamined, and continue to be held in the face of evidence that contradicts them. One of those assumptions was that students wanted to get good grades and would be motivated by this desire.

Ms. Bridgestone, perhaps because of her own background as a "good student" and her relative lack of familiarity (as a student teacher) with the students, placed a good deal of emphasis on grades, and her underlying assumption seemed to be that grades were important and students cared what their grades were. She wanted to use student concern about grades as a way to encourage them to accede to her agenda:

> Ms. Bridgestone begins writers' workshop with a discussion about grades. She tells the students that their interim report cards will be given out in three weeks, so in about two and a half weeks they will need to choose the best piece they have written, one that they think is really good, to be graded. One of the children asks if they can use their modern fairy tales as the graded piece, and Ms. Bridgestone checks with Ms. Corvo, who says yes, they can. Then they move on to a review of the steps in the writing process.

In Ms. Corvo's class, however, actual student concern with grades seems to be low. In the incident just described, Ms. Bridgestone is interrupted by student voices saying, "Interims? What's that?" Because these fifth graders were in an elementary school last year, this is their first year of experience with interim grades, but the upcoming grades will be their third set of interims. If they were concerned about their grades, they would have already learned what "interims" were.

Another incident confirms their lack of awareness of grades:

> Ms. Bridgestone is about to teach a lesson on writing the letter "k" correctly. She has noticed, she says, that many students are writing their "k's" so they look like "h's." She says that if they do this on their spelling test she will mark the words wrong and gives them an example of "remark" written "remarh."

> Ms. Bridgestone: There are four words like that [on the spelling list], so if you miss them all, what would your score be?
> Voices: D, C, B, 80 is a B, 80 is a C.
> Ms. Bridgestone: 80, that's right, so if you know all the words that would be 100, what, A+, but if you make these "h's" that would be a C. So I want you to use your paper to practice ... [Several groans are heard] writing the words three times each.

It is evident that the students are not very aware of the grading scale, and that they do not greet the opportunity to do something to improve their grades as a positive event.

It was rare in Ms. Corvo's class to see any evidence that students were concerned about grades or even felt competitive with one another in any way. During the oral reading, the worst readers were listened to as politely as the teacher, and the voice that supplied a word for a classmate who stumbled sounded helpful, rather than critical. The one such occurrence in the data was an interchange between a boy and two of his closest friends:

Thomas has been reading in partners with Peter. He goes up to the front of the room and walks past Andrew and Paul, who are reading together.

Thomas: *We're* finished. [implying, "and you are not."]

There is no response from Andrew and Paul.

Ms. Bridgestone also spent a good deal of time on an elaborate program for self-rating of student behavior that she called "Student of the Week." According to both Ms. Corvo and Ms. Bridgestone, it was quite ineffective in changing students' behavior. The essence of this system was to motivate the students to behave by offering them the chance to have their names posted on the door and to make their compliance at least in part a matter of their own responsibility rather than their response to the teacher. Lack of interest in who would be Student of the Week was obvious in the room when the weekly results were announced; it was also made clear by the fact that week after week the Students of the Week were already-well-behaved female students; students did not change their behavior to get this recognition. Meanwhile, Ms. Bridgestone's and Ms. Corvo's level of frustration with student behavior continued unabated.

Students Assuming Roles That Conflict With Teacher Expectations.

Students contributed to power relations by demanding various forms of adult attention or other privileges available from adults. Sometimes they were unsuccessful, as in this example from Ms. Kaminski's room:

The children are gathered on the rug.

Thad: (holding up a small object) I made this.

Ms. Kaminski ignores Thad and goes right on with what she is saying.

At other times, such efforts were effective:

It is readers' workshop time. Of all the children, only one boy is not involved with a book. Carlton is sitting on the rug with the squeaky raccoon puppet, looking at a book. He gets up and starts to push and pat the boy who does not have a book. The boy ignores him. Ms. Kaminski comes over to Carlton and takes him on her lap with the puppet. They read a book together.
Andra has made a picture of *The Very Hungry Caterpillar*. She shows it in turn to Ms. Kaminski, to the student teacher, and to the aide. Each of them stops what she is doing and says how great it is.

These kinds of actions seemed to fall within Ms. Kaminski's expectations for how children would behave, whether she commented on them or not. But sometimes students actually assumed a role outside her expectations, and this was often true of Erin:

Erin has written a story and wants to read it to the children. She does not just sit on the rug and do it, but sits in a chair next to the teacher and acts the teacher's part. She calls for quiet, asks everyone to put whatever they are holding on the floor in front of them, and calls several children to attention.
Children who have drawn or written something special can be taken to the teacher work room to photocopy or laminate their work. Erin seems to request this more often than anyone else. [I sense that she is pushing the limits of the adult's tolerance.]

Ms. Kaminski, at Erin's request, has written the date in Erin's notebook. Erin looks at it critically.

Erin: That's not a very good 2.
Ms. Kaminski: That's the kind of 2 that came out so that's how it will have to be.

Ms. Kaminski's awareness of the special role that Erin assumes in the room is revealed in this incident:

The students are in the process of gathering on the rug. Erin is sitting in Ms. Kaminski's rocking chair.

Ms. Kaminski: Erin, every time I have to ask you to get out of my chair at group time I am going to send you to sit at a table [away from the group].

Erin moves to an adjacent chair.

Ms. Kaminski: Why don't you sit on the rug *with the regular children?* (emphasis added)

Ms. Kaminski gently moves Erin down to the rug.

When Ms. Kaminski read about this incident in a transcript of my notes, she was shocked that she had used the phrase, "with the regular children." Yet she agreed that it expressed her feelings about Erin.

Carlton, another of Ms. Kaminski's students, frequently acts in similar ways, and Ms. Kaminski reacted similarly:

They are seated on the rug sharing the projects they did at home. Carlton jumps up.

Carlton: Ms. Kaminski, Ms. Kaminski, [Carlton almost never says her name just once] can I share?
Ms. Kaminski: No, not now, you have to raise your hand like everyone else.

STUDENTS ASSUMING THE ROLE OF THE TEACHER

The question of what is the teacher's role, and how it contrasts with those of the students, is of course one of the central uncertainties of this book. Yet, there were times when I saw student actions that both norms of behavior in American schools and educational research would assign to the teacher. These events, like those in direct conflict with teacher agendas, were relatively easy to observe.

Shared Control of Turn Taking

Hugh Mehan's well-known research on classroom interaction (1979), with its categories of Initiation, Response, and Evaluation, is based on the idea that it is up to the teacher to initiate turns to speak. Of the three categories, only Response consists of student speech; the opening and closing acts of Initiation and Evaluation belong to the teacher. In the classrooms I observed, it was certainly a frequent occurrence for the teacher to initiate a turn to speak, although I frequently saw several repetitions of Initiation and Response without an Evaluation (possibly the very act of turning to the next student with another question was a tacit evaluation, finding the response correct). However, it was also a frequent occurrence for students to take control of turn taking. (Griffin & Mehan, 1981, as well as Alpert, 1991, acknowledged the ability of students to take over the turn-assignment process.) To extend the central metaphor of this book, the control of turn taking (or control of the floor) could be thought of as process of laying a tile floor, made up of student-control tiles and teacher-control tiles, for the building called "What Teachers and Students Can Do Here."

Ms. Corvo and Ms. Bridgestone did not devote the entire language arts period to the highly structured and "seamless" activities described earlier.

The round-robin reading, for example, was interrupted regularly by questions and discussion topics raised by the teacher for the class. When Ms. Bridgestone asked a question, especially one that related the reading to the lives of the students, a space opened for student interaction. Commonly, such a question would be answered by one student who had raised a hand and been called on. This answer would be followed by a murmur of student voices commenting to one another on the question, the answer, and their feelings about it. As a rule, the teacher did not seem to be an intended hearer of these comments, and they were often ones that she might be expected to find more or less unacceptable. For example, from Ms. Corvo's room:

Student: I think Cybil [the heroine of the novel] is ugly.

In some cases, students became involved in such discussion to the point that they took over the floor, controlled the distribution of turns to talk, and influenced the definition of knowledge in the discussion. In this setting, though, if Ms. Bridgestone or Ms. Corvo wished to return to the structured turn taking of oral reading, she needed only to assign a reading turn. Talk would stop, students' bodies would return to positions within the parameters of the activity (see chap. 5), and student opportunities to control what was happening would be sharply reduced.

Even when Ms. Bridgestone was actually assigning turns, there were variations in the extent to which she controlled who would go next and when. Certainly there were times when her "Thank you, Donald. LaToya?" was the entire extent of the transition between turns, as Donald and LaToya and all the others complied passively. Ms. Bridgestone connected her task of assigning turns to her agenda for student learning by saying that she was trying to distribute the turns fairly while taking into consideration the fact that if a student reads really badly it is harder for the rest of the class to pay attention and to understand what is going on.

Yet there were many other times when students were waving their hands and calling out for turns, and Ms. Bridgestone selected from among those who were volunteering. Sometimes, this reached the level of actual negotiation:

Ms. Bridgestone: LaToya, you can read.
Andrew: She already read.
Ms. Bridgestone: You already read? Let's get someone who hasn't read. Andrew?

At other times, students designated themselves for turns, either in the context of the whole-class discussion or in subdiscussions that took place immediately after someone answered a teacher-asked question, or when the teacher had, for example, turned her back to the group to write on the board.

Ms. Kaminski, like Ms. Bridgestone, made some use of her power to assign turns to promote her agenda for student learning, making sure that children she thought would benefit from participation in a particular discussion or sharing time did get a turn. But as in the other classrooms, it was common for children to designate themselves for turns, or for the teacher to choose from among volunteers. Like Ms. Bridgestone, she was concerned with fairness in distributing turns, and on one occasion she said, "We'll have to make a signup sheet [for turns] so it will be fair."

Other Instances of Students Taking Over the Teacher's Roles

In Ms. Kaminski's room, I saw a number of incidents of students taking over teacher roles. One involved Carlton, an aggressive boy who often dominated in the classroom and who, in this case, tried to directly manipulate the teacher's prerogative of creating the physical environment.

Ms. Kaminski had created a space on the chalkboard called "computer signup list." Carlton tried to change that space:

It is early in the morning. Carlton arrives and shows off his ice cream money to some other students. Ms. Kaminski has written the words COMPUTER SIGNUP on the chalkboard behind the computer. Below the words, Nathaniel and Nick have written their names, indicating that they will be first and second. Nathaniel is using the computer and Nick is watching him. It appears that Carlton will have to be third.

But he gets a chair, pulls it up to the chalkboard, stands on it, and writes his name *above* the words COMPUTER SIGNUP. He gets down and tries to push Nathaniel out of the way, saying:

I'm first.

The student teacher comes over and reminds Carlton that they talked about this yesterday and he can't just push in. Carlton pulls up a chair to the computer and supervises Nathaniel as he continues to work.

Sometimes students, not prompted by their teacher to do so, offered assistance to other students who had made errors, during the course of a limited-response activity. These incidents also seemed to me to be cases in which students were taking over the teacher's role. In some classrooms, this might be part of the teacher's plan for the students; in Ms. Corvo's room, it was not encouraged by the teachers, but nevertheless happened often—probably in part because, as Ms. Bridgestone pointed out, it was hard to listen to the poorer readers during the regular round-robin reading:

Rosie reads with extreme difficulty. She reads "taking" for "talking."

LaToya: [quietly] Talking.

Rosie repeats, "talking," and goes on.
Soon Andrew helps her in the same way.
Hugh reads. He misreads the word "contestant," and murmurs of correc-
tion can be heard from around the group.
Andrew reads. He stumbles on the word "gratitude" and LaToya turns to
him and supplies the word.

STUDENT DEVELOPMENT
OF INTERACTIONAL SPACE

More frequent than instances of direct confrontation, especially in Ms.
Anderson's and Ms. Kaminski's rooms, were instances in which students
kept their actions out of direct conflict with the teacher's agenda. Just as
the teachers did through their use of time and space as well as politeness
and indirect discourse, students maintained the public agenda of cooperation. At the edges of the metaphorical structure of classroom power relations, and often at the edges of physical space and of the time assigned to
various activities, they found room for the actions that kept their day
interesting.

For example, as soon as the teacher's attention was distracted from them,
their level of interaction and action rose substantially. Some examples from
Ms. Corvo's classroom:

Ms. Corvo is at the front of the room, speaking to the students. She goes to
the back of the room to get something she needs from her desk. At once,
many of the kids start to fool around. Walter and Terrell are dueling with their
pencils. LaToya is punching Terrell in the arm. The noise level rises as students
all over the room start to talk.
Ms. Bridgestone is getting ideas from students and writing them on the
chalkboard. Every time she turns her back the noise level rises.

The end point of each of the day's structured activities was another such
opportunity. For example, the transition after the spelling test was signalled
by the teacher:

Ms. Bridgestone: V-a-c-u-u-m. Anybody else? Save the paper; you can use it
to study from.

Immediately things just seem to break loose. Three students are out of
their seats, two are shooting wads of paper into the trash can, and numerous

voices can be heard, in sharp contrast to the control and silence of the last ten minutes.

During writers' workshop in Ms. Corvo's room, there is a fair amount of legitimate opportunity to move around the room, to and from conferences and the "publishing area." It is not too hard for a student to spend a good part of writers' workshop more or less wandering around, and some students, such as Hugh and Donald, are expert at this. Ms. Corvo and Ms. Bridgestone are concerned about this behavior, and have some strategies to control it:

> Ms. Corvo: No one's talking. No one needs to get out of their seats. No one needs to conference. We did that too much yesterday.

But students continue to find spaces within the room and within the writing workshop in which to carry on conversations and to move around—and in this classroom, the teachers' agenda of controlling student behavior definitely seeks to put firm limits on moving around.

In Ms. Corvo's classroom times such as these were small slices of opportunity; students were most often under the teacher's gaze and had little chance to develop their own space for interaction. In Ms. Kaminski's room, however, there was so much going on in the room, so many things, so many children moving around actively, that it did not seem to be possible for the adults (Ms. Kaminski, the aide, the student teacher, possibly the reading teacher, and any volunteers who might be present) to see what all the children were doing all the time. This was especially likely because these adults usually saw their role as one of being actively involved in promoting learning with one or more children, rather than being in a supervisory role over the room at large. Thus, there was a lot of space around the edges of adult attention, and students used that space. (Probably uneasiness with the idea of students using this unsupervised space is a factor in some teachers' resistance to "open classroom" arrangements like Ms. Kaminski's.)

Most of the time, just as in Ms. Corvo's room, a majority of the students were doing what they were supposed to be doing. That meant that at free choice time they were engaged with one of the acceptable choices, at readers' workshop time they were involved in some way with a book, and at writers' workshop time they were writing. When they were supposed to be sitting on the rug and listening, most of them were. Yet, much of the time someone was *not* complying, and most of the children were that someone at times.

For example, during my first observation in the classroom, the following events occurred during readers' workshop:

> One boy in the library corner is kicking another boy, not very hard, but with big shoes. The other sits up and punches him, also not very hard, which seems

to end the problem. No one seems to notice this.
A boy has the squeaky raccoon puppet and is playing noisily with it on the
rug.
There is tickling and rolling around on the rug.
One boy is playing noisily on the rug with Mandy, who has a book. The two
push one another and he makes loud, silly noises.
Buster is sitting on the rocking chair and scooting it around the rug.

Nothing harmful was going on, but there was a good deal happening that
did not fit in with the teacher's intentions for this time—that everyone
would interact with printed material in some way that would promote
learning. Later in the year, as expectations were better established and more
children felt able to engage productively with written matter, there was less
of this kind of student activity—but usually some of it.

Even during group times, children in Ms. Kaminski's room might be able
to find space in which they were, at least for a time, unnoticed:

The children are gathered in the library corner to be shown the new books
that have been put out. Ms. Kaminski is standing to one side, holding up
books and talking to the students. More or less behind her, Thad is crawling
around on the floor, scooting a little wad of paper around. He is obviously
paying no attention to what Ms. Kaminski is doing. After about four
minutes, Ms. Kaminski seems to notice him for the first time and tells him
to join the group on the rug.
Ms. Kaminski chooses Mandy to read aloud. Buster and Pearl are sitting
next to each other on the rug. They have a magazine and are reading or
looking at it.

Sunny Kaminski: Pearl …

A few moments later Pearl is still reading the magazine while Mandy reads
aloud.

In Ms. Anderson's room, where students and teacher colluded most
successfully on the agenda of cooperation, it was still common for interaction levels to rise between activities:

They go on to cross-correcting their math homework. There is a lot of chatter
and children are out of their seats between this and the previous activity, yet
when Ms. Anderson is ready to go it stops at once.

The most outstanding example in her room of this kind of student use of
unsupervised moments was something I did *not* see—in fact, it probably
would not have occurred if I had happened to be there:

I ask Ms. Anderson about the fact that the desks are in rows today, rather than in the more usual clusters. She says that yesterday afternoon she had bus duty and therefore left the room two minutes before the students were dismissed. When she returned, the children were gone and there were crayons everywhere—a crayon fight [throwing crayons] had taken place. She said that putting the desks in rows, without giving the students a choice about where to sit, was a way of showing how upset she was about this.

Later, I asked Vincent about this incident, and he said only a few had been throwing crayons. Still, even this generally restrained class was capable of quite an outbreak when Ms. Anderson was not with them.

STUDENT STRATEGIES TO MAKE TEACHER CONTROL VISIBLE AND CHALLENGING

Although actions through which students made the teachers' control visible, so that it could be challenged, were rare, they were relatively dramatic. These were instances in which students attempted to force into the open an issue that the teacher apparently would have preferred to keep submerged. The following extended incident from Ms. Bridgestone's classroom serves to illustrate this possibility for student action:

LaToya has a reading turn. She reads smoothly and with some expression. At the end of the turn, Ms. Bridgestone asks her a question about what she has read. Her answer is incorrect, and Ms. Bridgestone supplies the correct answer. LaToya's facial expression reveals that she is not pleased that this happened. [She is one of the stronger students in the class, and rarely gives a wrong answer.]

Ms. Bridgestone takes a reading turn, and then starts a discussion about a boy in the book who says that his parents lie to him all the time. LaToya stands up and goes to the trash can. [This is a clear violation of expectations during oral reading.]

Ms. Bridgestone: Sit down, LaToya.

LaToya sits back down with obvious irritation.
A minute or two later, LaToya asks if she can go to the bathroom.
Ms. Bridgestone says no.
LaToya mumbles something under her breath.
Meanwhile, Donald is talking loudly. Ms. Bridgestone tells him to go to his isolated seat.
Donald refuses.

Ms. Bridgestone waits quietly. Then she goes over to him and talks in a low voice. He answers quietly, and she says:

Then you'll have to go to detention.

Ms. Bridgestone walks over to the teacher's desk to get a detention slip, and Donald sits back down where he is.

LaToya: (softly) Detention ain't no shit.

Ms. Bridgestone asks the class for attention. All but LaToya turn quietly toward her.
LaToya has turned around in her seat and is talking to Darin.
Ignoring this, Ms. Bridgestone proceeds with the lesson.
Within two minutes, LaToya is apparently focused on the lesson, raises her hand, and answers a question correctly.

In an interview, Ms. Bridgestone referred to this incident as the realization of her worst fears that she would someday have a confrontation with the students, that they would refuse to do what she asked, but she was pleased with the outcome. However, it was the only time that I saw her wield her school-sanctioned disciplinary power in the classroom (by threatening Donald with a detention)—a rare event in any of these classrooms and one that all the teachers tried to avoid.
Students also sometimes refused to accept the polite or indirect discourse that was being offered to them and instead required the teacher to make a more direct statement. In this way they forced the teacher's agenda to the surface so that they could oppose it. They prevented the teacher from maintaining the pretense that what was going on was cooperation and mutual politeness. For example, in Ms. Corvo's room:

Lewis was slow to start writing.

Ms. Bridgestone: It's best to use a pen. [meaning: use a pen]
Lewis: Do I have to use a pen? Ms. Bridgestone: Yes, Lewis, you have to use a pen.
Lewis: But I don't like to because ...

Ms. Bridgestone has passed out a worksheet that the students are supposed to do. She looks down at Donald, who is sitting right next to her, and says:

Donald, will you please read the directions?

Donald: I don't want to.
Ms. Bridgestone: [with a surprised look] You don't want to? Well, OK.

She reads the instructions.

It was clear that the children knew the difference, that they were not in reality deceived by the politeness formulas used by the teachers. If they acceded to them, it was by their own choice, or as McDermott and Tylbor (1986) would say, their own collusion. The following example illustrates this point very clearly:

Ms. Bridgestone consistently ended reading turns by saying, "Thank you." The student who had been reading would stop, and Ms. Bridgestone would comment on what had been read or raise a question for discussion or say the name of the next student to read (e.g., "Lewis?"). In this case, Donald was reading.

Ms. Bridgestone: Thank you, Donald. [meaning, stop].

Donald went right on reading.
LaToya was sitting behind Donald.

LaToya: [in a fierce whisper] She said you can stop.

Donald finished the sentence he was reading and stopped.

It is not easy to say why Donald went on reading. He may not have heard Ms. Bridgestone; it is possible, but unlikely (McDermott & Roth, 1978), that he did not know what "thank you" meant in this context. There was nothing about his tone of voice or facial expression that suggested he was refusing. What is very clear, though, is that LaToya understood both the meaning ("you should stop") of what was said and the place of the teacher's politeness formula in a power relationship, as shown by the tone of her command to Donald. She was speaking to him in the voice that the teacher would not use, the voice of authority.

An important theme in Ms. Anderson's room was "using positive language," as she called it. This seemed to mean that both students and teachers were using many indirect discourse strategies and politeness formulas. But even she could be pushed into revealing openly the fact that she, and not the class, was making a decision:

Ms. Anderson gives instructions for what they will do next. A group of boys who are sitting together are not paying attention, and she repeats the instructions three times before she gets cooperation. [This is very unusual in this room, in my experience.] She tells the boys what is bothering her about the situation, and restates the purpose of the boys' sitting together. One of the boys starts to defend what happened, and she interrupts him:

> I'm not looking for input. I'm telling you how I'm feeling. I'm willing to continue with this if you can do the agreement.

The agenda of cooperation was maintained without resistance in this much more typical event:
When Vincent starts to read there is a buzz of talk.
Ms. Anderson stops and says:

> Excuse me, Vincent, may I interrupt?

She turns to William and Kevin, who were talking.

> Ms. Anderson: Boys, it's really hard for me to listen over here (gestures toward Vincent) when there's noise over there.

The noise stops.

A good deal of effort on the teachers' part goes into maintaining the collaborated-on agenda of mutual cooperation and courtesy. The ways that teachers use time and space (chap. 5) and their predominant use of politeness formulas and indirect discourse strategies (chap. 6) testify to their investment in maintaining this agenda. So, it is a significant event when students are able to disrupt teachers' careful efforts to conceal their agendas of controlling student actions.

* * *

In all three classrooms, students' contributions to the construction of power relationships were most often quite direct. They seemed to seek either to develop spaces within the teacher-built structure in which they could act freely, or to develop spaces in which the teachers had to act according to their wishes. Occasionally, they attempted to upset the teachers' strategies of indirection and invisibility in order to make possible a direct conflict over the teachers' agendas. Their contributions to the building of the "What Teachers and Students Can Do Here" structure were substantial and probably impossible for teachers to prevent.

Teachers like Ms. Corvo spend large amounts of effort seeking to control and limit student actions in the belief that they should be the holders of power in the classrooms, and that student contributions to power relations are a form of insurrection against the legitimate government of the classroom. Their efforts, however, seem only to increase students' motivation to resist, to disrupt, and to bring teachers' agendas into the open.

Regardless of whether teachers seek to exercise sole control of classroom power (like Ms. Corvo), or whether they actively intend to share authority with their students (like Ms. Kaminski and Ms. Anderson), students will make their own contributions to the development of classroom power relations. To quote Nel Noddings (1995), "In a real and ultimate sense, teachers do not have control over what students do—unless they are willing to use the methods of a drill sergeant or one who 'washes brains' through physical and emotional coercion" (p. 75).

This is a reality of classroom interaction, and teachers will be more comfortable in their classrooms if they accept, rather than resist, the interactive nature of classroom power relations.

Chapter 9

How Is It Useful to Look at Classrooms in This Way?

      ଚ   ◆   ଓ

The last four chapters of this book have explored several questions in the context of an interactive constructivist theory of power relations:

- How do teacher choices about the physical organization of classrooms and the kinds of activities that take place in them contribute to the construction of power relations?
- Why and how do teachers cloak their contributions to power relations behind politeness formulas and indirect discourse strategies?
- What kinds of student and teacher actions contribute to defining what is to count as classroom knowledge in a particular classroom at a particular time?
- What student actions can be understood as being in conflict with teachers' arrangements of classroom time and space?
- What student actions can be understood as seeking to make the teachers's agenda visible so it can be challenged?
- What kinds of student actions can be understood as their efforts to create areas within power relations in which they can act freely?

The study on which this book is based makes a start at answering such questions, and suggests what kinds of analysis can produce more complete answers. The individual qualities of the three classrooms, with their teachers and students, as described in chapters 2, 3, and 4, must be kept in mind in thinking about the details of the analysis. The study belongs to a research genre that calls on readers to make judgments about the validity of its conclusions. By providing "thick description" (Geertz, 1973) of the three classrooms and of the events and actions included in the analysis, I have tried to provide readers with enough information to make a sound judgment as to validity.

Yet even if readers find discrepancies between my analysis of the classrooms described here and their own experiences, suggestions as to what kinds of things to look for in classrooms may be of use in many situations. Discourse strategies selected by teachers and students, use of indirect speech acts, competition and grades, control of turn taking, choices of physical organization and of activities by teachers, and student actions in response to such choices can be observed everywhere; questions about how they are connected to power relations in classrooms can always be raised.

Many different aspects of these three classrooms seem likely to have affected what I observed. For example, these were three quite peaceful classrooms in quite peaceful schools. None of them resembled urban schools where I have worked, in which many classrooms were often scenes of overt conflict. Doubtless different kinds of actions would have been seen in schools where conflicts between teachers and students were stronger and more visible.

All three teachers were White females (like a majority of teachers, especially elementary teachers, today). The role of the teacher's gender and ethnicity in affecting how teachers contribute to power relations, and how students respond to them, was not available for exploration. On the one hand, each of the classrooms was ethnically diverse, and included students from varied socioeconomic classes. On the other hand, differences attributable to ethnicity or class might be more obvious in classrooms that were more uniform in either or both of these areas.

Also, these classrooms were all at the elementary level and one included very young children. It seems possible that different kinds of actions on the part of both students and teachers would be seen in secondary classrooms. One might guess that older students would bring to their actions more of the deliberately strategic quality that sometimes appeared in this study in the actions of the teachers. They might be more aware, too, of likely responses to their actions and more likely to consciously collude with one another in opposition to the teacher's agenda.

Still, I have found many of the ideas presented in this book relevant in my own graduate classes, where I work with practicing teachers with an average of 12 years in the classroom, and in undergraduate classrooms where I work with a mixture of traditional-aged and older students. In our culture, there is an overarching similarity of structure among almost all kinds of classrooms. That similarity makes it possible to extend the observations in this book to classrooms beyond the three in which the observations took place.

* * *

The ideas discussed in this book have implications for three overlapping groups of readers: teachers, teacher educators, and educational researchers. The rest of this chapter addresses each group in turn.

IMPLICATIONS FOR TEACHERS

How does it affect teachers to spend their days in this dance of conflicting and colluded-on, obvious and concealed agendas? Can an analysis like this be helpful to teachers, as they reflect on what they do and why they do it, or does it only add a layer to the already confusing tissue of classroom interaction? Can teachers benefit from understanding the play of agendas as they deal with students who are seeking to carry out their own agendas even while they either collaborate with teachers on an agreed-on public agenda, or seek to make the teacher's agenda visible so that it can be challenged?

There are at least four areas in which the analysis in this book can, I believe, help teachers in their classroom life. The first has to do with the linkage between power and responsibility. The second concerns teachers' thinking about providing choices for students, or what is often called "sharing authority" (Oyler, 1996). The third has to do with the connection between classroom management and making choices about teaching and learning, and the fourth is about the value of careful looking at events in classrooms.

Power and Responsibility

Both the literature of classroom management and our cultural conception of what school is like envision teachers as having great power in the classroom, and therefore great responsibility for all aspects of life in their classrooms. If the buck can be said to stop anywhere in the complex web of relationships that link students, families, administrators, political figures, educational specialists, and teachers, it stops with teachers.

This statement is confirmed by the continuing focus by many educational reformers on the selection, education, and evaluation of teachers. Such reformers promise that the route to improvement of schooling is through the improvement of teachers. Politicians of the last 15 years, commenting on various showings that American children are not learning, have insisted that this is because their teachers are inadequate, or at least are pursuing incorrect policies. As I was completing this chapter, my local newspaper carried this quotation from North Carolina governor James B. Hunt, Jr., chair of the National Commission on Teaching and America's Future: "If we get the teachers right, everything else will follow" ("Overhaul," 1996).

It exemplifies the emphasis on teacher responsibility that has been the centerpiece of reform efforts in recent years.

This heavy load of responsibility seems to be one of the factors that make teaching such a stressful and demanding job. An elementary teacher with 25 children in her classroom bears a responsibility for them far more intense than that of a doctor with 25 patients or a manager with 25 employees. For 6 or 7 hours a day, day after day, the teacher is expected to construct every detail of the students' environment, to control the context in which they live and work. She is supposed to ensure that the students will learn, will want to learn, and will learn effectively what is necessary so that they can become scientists, technicians, responsible citizens, informed voters, competent readers, clear writers, and more. Secondary teachers, though usually held responsible for a narrower range of student learning, bear full responsibility for that range for far higher numbers of students.

This heavy load of responsibility is increased for the teacher who is urged to use methods of direct instruction that center accountability for student learning ever more clearly on the teacher. More and more often, teachers are evaluated either with instruments that test their possession of skills that are "known to result in student learning" or on the basis of tests that are assumed to measure student learning. When teachers are held fully accountable for student learning, as if they were wholly in control of everything that happens in their classrooms, they are placed under unnecessary and unfair stress. Their complaints that they are unable to do what they are asked to do are often dismissed as whining.

Schools and teachers have responded to this excessive centering of responsibility on the teacher in a number of ways. One is to hand off some of the responsibility to "experts," by adopting teaching materials that more or less guarantee that if the teacher uses them correctly they will result in students' learning and wanting to learn. If the students do not learn, however, the responsibility may still be presumed to lie with the teacher, as the materials were supposed to be foolproof. One of my students, a middle school teacher in an inner-city neighborhood where students and their families bore the burden of many complex problems in their out-of-school lives, complained to a curriculum specialist in her field that the biggest problem she had in her classroom was student absences. The specialist told her that if she taught her subject correctly, as she had been taught through the specialist's in-services, the students would all come to school. This was despite the fact that the students had many teachers in the middle school, as well as the fact that what is happening at home is often the strongest influence on student attendance in school. It is a clear instance of the kind of unreasonable centering of responsibility on teachers and their methods that I find so inappropriate.

Another way to resist this centering of responsibility on the teacher is to label certain children as not able to learn or as in need of specialist treatment if learning is to take place. The teacher cannot be held responsible for the learning of such children, so her responsibility is decreased. Teachers' resistance to the inclusion movement may have a great deal to do with their fear that responsibility for the learning of students identified as having special needs will be returned to them. Labeling students with disabilities at least succeeds in reducing some of the regular education teacher's load of responsibility, and even the special education teacher is in a position to claim that students do not learn because they cannot, rather than because the teacher has failed.

Neither of these efforts to reduce teachers' level of responsibility by reducing their area of competency seems to have helped children learn more or teachers feel less burdened. Teachers still struggle with everyone's expectations that whatever happens, they are responsible for all classroom outcomes. And students continue to be harmed by being labeled as *disabled*, while they are denied the benefits of the kind of locally developed curriculum that many believe leads to maximum learning.

What is the effect on teachers of this excessive load of responsibility? Different individuals respond differently. Some become exhausted and choose to leave teaching. Some seek more and more control over their students, regimenting their classrooms more and more severely in an effort to meet the responsibilities they have been assigned. Behavior control, rather than learning, becomes the central focus of their work. Others are simply overwhelmed by what is asked of them. Many people remember a childhood experience with a teacher—or perhaps have been a teacher—who burst into tears or ran from the room because the students were "out of control." None of these responses is helpful for either teachers or students.

This book offers an understanding of classroom life based on an interactive and constructivist understanding of power relationships. It suggests viewing classrooms in a way that greatly reduces the level of psychological responsibility teachers have to bear. If classrooms are understood as places where a group of individuals, a teacher and some students, together construct what happens, what can happen, what is possible and what is impossible, what gets learned and what doesn't, then the teacher cannot be solely responsible for classroom outcomes. Teachers can shift their focus from achieving tight control of student behavior to making a positive contribution to the development of power relations in the classrooms where they live and work.

The teacher's institutional role allows planning the physical arrangements of the classroom and the kinds of activities that will take place, but students' actions are constantly shaping what the teacher does and can do even in this arena of action. Similarly, the teacher's role is assumed to be that of arbiter of knowledge in the classroom; texts and materials used and teaching techniques chosen are said to define what will count as knowledge.

But students' actions constantly shape and define what will count as classroom knowledge, whether or not the teacher invites their participation in that process.

At first glance, it would seem that each individual in an interactional context can choose to perform whatever actions will promote her or his agenda. In reality, those choices will be constrained by agendas shared by all members (agendas constituted through the actions and response of others) and by the actions of others that constitute their private agendas. These constraints are as real for teachers (who cannot avoid being members of the group that lives together in a classroom) as they are for students. They are the functions of power relations that have been constructed and are constantly under construction in the classroom.

This understanding of the workings of classroom life has the potential to lift some of the burden of responsibility from the backs of teachers. It acknowledges the reality that in a world of interactive relationships, of interactive construction of power relationships in particular, no one person can control everything that happens to a group of people. No one can fairly say to teachers, "You are in charge. If you cannot accomplish what you are supposed to accomplish, something is wrong with you."

This is not to imply that the teacher who accepts this interactive understanding of classroom life must simply give up the task of promoting student learning in the classroom. The teacher is an important member of the classroom group, with an institutional role supporting actions that make a large contribution to the shape of power relations constructed in the classroom. In many cases, students' acceptance of that institutional role will be part of the baggage they carry to school and will be actualized in their actions in the classroom, increasing the teacher's ability to shape power relationships as they are constructed and revised.

Still, teachers can not be the locus of all responsibility. Even as they seek to promote the agendas they bring to the classroom, teachers will also be able to acknowledge that all their actions are constituted by, just as they constitute, power relations to which they are only contributors. This transformation of teachers' views of the classrooms they live in has the potential to relieve the frustration that is encouraged by accepting total responsibility for so much that cannot be controlled.

A number of writers (e.g., Sedlak et al., 1986; Sizer, 1984; and Metz, 1990) have suggested that many teachers have shifted their focus too strongly to the public agenda of cooperation, to their desire to maintain positive interpersonal relations with their students. If teachers have abandoned their agenda of control of student behavior in order to facilitate student learning, it is because the expectation that they will control student behavior is so strong. This outcome is not what should result from acceptance by teachers of the interactive nature of classroom power relationships; on the contrary, teachers who understand that they are constructing power relations with their students will be able to focus more clearly on the learning they want to see.

To acknowledge that power relationships in classrooms are constructed interactively is not to abandon one's own agenda for the classroom. Instead, it is to accept that one's own agenda will usually be one of a number of competing agendas, all of which will be actualized in the construction of power relationships. One cannot expect one's agenda to prevail unchallenged in the classroom or elsewhere. It is also to accept that one's own agenda will be shaped by the agendas and actions of others in the classroom, whether those of other staff or those of students.

To understand the sources and consequences of observed actions is to have the potential either to change them or to respond differently to them. Suppose a teacher realizes, for example, that the discourse she or he chooses is not only performing a routine communicative task, such as "politely asking the students to prepare for the next activity of the day," but is also making a specifiable contribution to the construction of power relationships. The teacher might weigh the choices he or she is making more thoughtfully and perhaps promote a self-defined agenda more successfully.

When the teacher is dealing with a student who does not seem to grasp her or his intentions, it might be helpful to consider the possibility that the student is making a more or less deliberate effort to challenge the teacher's agenda. Then, the teacher might be able to respond to the student's intention rather than to the "misunderstanding" that appears to be taking place—a waste of time and energy if the student actually understands perfectly well what the teacher wants. (See Kohl, 1995, for an extended discussion of situations like this.)

As teachers live in classrooms with their students, their understanding of the nature of classroom interaction is likely to be transmitted to the students. Teachers' actions will be different just because they are not seeking ever-increasing control over the actions of their students. They are likely to leave more openings in which students can pursue their personal agendas, and to choose different discourse strategies from those they would use if they were seeking complete control.

In response, students may pursue their own agendas in more positive ways, spending less time in conflict with their teachers and more time in cooperative and independent modes of action. Classrooms are in trouble when negative student–teacher relationships take time and attention away from learning, and it seems possible that a changed understanding of classroom relationships by the teacher, when transmitted through the teacher's actions to the students, would help to improve the tone of these relationships.

Noddings (1991) called for schools "in which teachers and students live together, talk together, reason together, take delight in each other's company" (p. 169). It seems possible that the development of such interpersonal relationships in schools would be facilitated by the changed understanding of the nature of classroom power relations discussed here. How can teachers relate to students in the ways Noddings called for if they believe (as does Waller) that they are engaged in a battle in which if the teacher does not win, "he [sic] cannot remain a teacher?" (1965, p. 196).

In talking about these matters, it is easy, as always, to sound as though the whole responsibility is still with teachers. The argument may be taken to suggest that if only teachers would understand power relationships differently, they could solve classroom problems better. This is not what is intended. Instead, I suggest that a different understanding of power relationships may help to make teachers' work less difficult, and if carried over to students may help to create more positive relations in the classroom. There is still room for the case in which, for example, student agendas are so intensely in conflict with those of the school and the teacher that positive relations continue to be impossible. The responsibility for such difficult situations is what should not rest directly on the teacher.

Choices for Students

A point that has been made again and again in the earlier chapters of this book is that when teachers organize their classrooms in ways that provide many choices for students, they are not thereby giving up their agendas of controlling student behavior to promote student learning. Some teachers—presented with curricular reforms like whole language, integrative curriculum, writing and reading workshops, and the multiple intelligences classroom—feel it is inappropriate to "turn over control to the students." How will they be able to assume responsibility for what is happening in their classrooms (as institution and culture expect them to) if they are not making all the decisions? I think this question is based on a misperception of what actually happens in classrooms when teachers adopt these curricular ideas.

First, as discussed in the preceding section, teachers never are totally in control of what happens in their classrooms. Students have agendas that they are enacting just as much as the teacher has hers. For example, careful observation of Aileen Corvo's classroom, where she (along with Courtney Bridgestone) intended to be very much in control, showed a multiplicity of ways that children were making their own contributions to power relationships.

Second, it is also true that teachers who believe that giving choices to students will enhance their learning, and who allow students to choose the books they will read, the topics they will write about, the activities they will engage in, or even the subjects the entire class will study, are actively pursuing the teacher agenda of controlling student behavior to promote student learning. For example, Sunny Kaminski provided a broad range of learning activities during free choice time, as well as a narrower but still substantial range during readers' and writers' workshops, and filled her classroom's shelves with books and other learning materials from which students could choose. Sue Anderson asked students to choose both the Native American nation whose history they would study and the ways in which they would express what they learned. Even Aileen Corvo and Courtney Bridgestone allowed students to write about violence and gangs during writers' workshop. All these decisions were made because each teacher believed that making these choices would help students learn more and learn better.

Even though Ms. Corvo and Ms. Bridgestone had qualms about the appropriateness of the topics the students chose, they were committed to the model of writing workshop that stresses the learning benefits of student choice of topics, and their belief in those benefits underlay their decision not to interfere with student choices. It was their desire for students to learn that shaped their decision, rather than their understandable uneasiness about what this class of fifth graders chose to write about. Similarly, Sunny Kaminski and Sue Anderson both clearly articulated their belief that the choices they were giving would in themselves enhance student learning.

Thus, the analysis of classroom interaction in this book indicates that teachers need not fear that offering student choices is inappropriate to their institutional role—as long as they offer those choices on the basis of what they believe about teaching and learning.

Classroom Management and Beliefs About Teaching and Learning

A related implication of this study is the strong connection it suggests between teachers' decisions about classroom management and teachers' beliefs about teaching and learning. It is often at the beginning of a teacher's career that these two matters become separated. Leaving a teacher preparation program full of the latest ideas about curriculum and instruction—whatever those may be—new teachers are often confronted with classroom management problems they feel unprepared to deal with. A common response is to leave behind the new curricular ideas, labeling them unrealistic, and allow their need to control student behavior to overshadow their need to promote student learning. They may set patterns of classroom interaction in these early years that will leave them forever unable to adapt to ideas for curriculum change and reform—or even ideas for change in classroom management.

This book suggests that classroom management and beliefs about teaching and learning can be seen as a seamless whole, contributing to the same teaching agenda. Teachers need to evaluate their efforts to control student behavior in terms of whether those efforts are promoting student learning—because student learning is the purpose of such control. The answer to such an evaluation question has to lie with the individual teacher, at least initially, and others may disagree with it. But to separate these two matters is to lose sight of the fact that education—schooling—is about learning, not about behavior control.

Careful Looking

A fourth implication of this study for teachers is that by observing both themselves and their students carefully and thinking about the relationship between their actions and their agendas, new understandings of what is going on in the classroom can be found. The premise of this study is that every action by a member in the classroom is a contribution to the construction of power relations. Understanding of what is happening in the classroom may be facilitated by highlighting some of those actions. Student comments, teacher movements, people saying "please" and "thank you," all the trivial events of classroom life, often blur into an undifferentiated haze of activity. By focusing on particular actions and how they serve as materials for the construction of power relations, clearer understanding of events may be reached.

A study such as this requires careful and extended observation of children and teachers in classrooms. Such observation may seem like a luxury that busy teachers cannot afford. Yet, if teachers reading this study find the analysis of student actions—and their own actions—in this way to be a useful tool for understanding the construction of power relations in their classrooms, they may find ways to make similar observations in their own situations.

Cultivating an observing attitude, so that at least some of the individual events that occur are noticed, is a good beginning for such observations. Even in the heat of classroom interaction, teachers can focus on their own actions, or on the actions of students, in a way that foregrounds just a few events for later reflection. Also, teachers can use some of the quieter times in their classrooms, perhaps when students are engaged in reading or writing, to look carefully at what is happening. Other possibilities include audiotaping or videotaping an occasional time period, and then viewing or listening with questions about the meaning of actions recorded.

It is true that such observing may seem easier in a classroom in which student actions are tightly controlled, so that the range of activity at any one time is narrower and easier to see. As discussed in chapter 8, in a classroom like Sunny Kaminski's, where students are often on the move and interacting around the edges of adult attention, it is impossible for a teacher to see everything that is happening at any one time, let alone to focus on it for later reflection. Unease with this reality is surely at the root of some teachers' resistance to establishing such classrooms. Yet, it was clear to me, as a full-time observer in each of these three classrooms (and many others), that it is never possible to see everything, that selection is necessary. Even with a video camera, which presumably records everything that happens in its range of vision, analysis has to be either incomplete or limited to brief time periods because it takes so much longer than the events themselves. In accepting the understanding of classroom reality considered in this book, teachers need to accept that they are never seeing every detail of the classroom picture.

IMPLICATIONS FOR TEACHER EDUCATORS

In addition to the outcomes for teachers previously discussed, there are two aspects of this study that speak to teacher educators. One is the need it uncovers for self-study by them as teachers in their own classrooms. The other is the importance of emphasizing the connections between classroom management and teaching and learning decisions, as discussed earlier. Too often issues of content and methods are instructionally separated from those of classroom management, often in separate courses. Students fail to gain a sense of the intimate relationship between the two kinds of decisions that they will be making in their classrooms, and the need to constantly evaluate classroom management for its effects on student learning.

Self-Study

Because I am a teacher/educator myself, entering the classroom with groups of practicing and future teachers week after week, it is natural that I have thought about the implications of this study for my own teaching. Trying to cultivate an observing eye in my own classroom, and seeking opportunities to reflect with my peers on what I have learned and observed, I have become more and more aware that power relations in my classroom work in the same ways as in the classrooms I studied. Often this knowledge has been helpful in understanding how to work most successfully with a particular student or situation.

Those individual choices are too specific to deal with here. However, the general concept that has become most important to me is the recognition that my classroom management choices need to be closely linked with my beliefs about teaching and learning, just as I suggest that those of classroom teachers must be. This recognition requires intensive self-study, leading to an examination of every aspect of my classroom actions. From the way I arrange the seating in my classroom, to the ways that I and the class together decide to use our time, to the assessment methods we use, to the way we develop assignments, every item of classroom action becomes subject to scrutiny.

Ties Between Curriculum and Classroom Management

Teachers need to understand the close relationship between control of student behavior and promoting student learning. Acknowledging and emphasizing this linkage would lead to changes in many teacher-education courses. The task of equipping teachers with a clear understanding of how student learning can be promoted in classrooms is only a beginning. Teaching the philosophy and practice of whole language, integrated curriculum, hands-on science, and problem-centered mathematics is not enough.

If teacher educators want teachers to apply what they have learned in their real-life classrooms, they need to focus on the connection between curriculum and classroom management, between the "controlling student behavior" and "promoting student learning" parts of their agendas. Field experiences and observations need to be carefully processed to unearth difficulties and practice problem-solving while the student is still in the supportive environment of the teacher-education classroom. Student teachers need to develop a habit of asking how a proposed solution to a difficulty involving student behavior relates to the learning they would like to seek on the part of their own students.

These practices are essential to help teachers avoid being in the position of one of my students who teaches mathematics in an inner-city middle school. "I know they're not learning," she said, referring to her students. "But I'm afraid to do what I know I should because I don't know what to do if they get out of control." She had attended many classes on how to introduce manipulatives, cooperative groups, and real-life connections to her math classroom, and she was a believer in their value. But whatever help she had received in connecting curricular to management issues had not been sufficient to allow her to pursue student learning as a primary agenda.

EDUCATIONAL RESEARCHERS

For researchers, who of course may be either teachers or teacher educators, the central implication of this study is what it says about what the focus of research should be. Much educational research is strongly action-oriented. It usually aims not just to learn about educational settings, but to discover choices or changes that can improve some aspect of education. It seeks to learn how to "do" education better. Therefore, the educational researcher takes a point of view that will lead to effective action.

Whether tacitly or not, the researcher asks, "Where does power lie in this setting?" and works from that vantage point. For the action-oriented researcher, what good can result from choosing a research viewpoint from which effective change cannot originate? This quality of educational research makes the question of where power is found in the classroom a critical one. If studies are to be conducted from the location of power, researchers must know what that location will be, and must also understand how power operates in the classroom.

The question of where power is found has not received a definitive answer from educational researchers; its location is thought to depend on the particular interaction being considered. Gamoran and Dreeben (1986), for example, held that the physical environment of schools is controlled by central administration, personnel decisions by building administrators, allocation of time by central and building administrators and teachers (though teachers are seen as having a late and negative effect, as they subvert administrative decisions), and curricular materials by central administration and teachers (who supplement or modify the curriculum "in the absence of supervision"). Clearly, researchers espousing this view of school life would locate their research primarily in the area of policy, seeking to influence the actions of administrators.

Other kinds of studies locate power in the society or culture at large, and seek to understand how larger structures influence schools. The aim of these researchers might be to find ways of influencing those larger structures, or of changing the way in which schools respond to them.

Others, taking a psychological point of view, try to observe the inner processes of teachers or students, seeing the classroom from inside their heads. Some of these (e.g., Bruner, 1966; Vygotsky, 1986; and Donaldson, 1978) have studied children's thinking, or, like Myra and David Sadker (1994), have pursued questions concerning teacher and student ideas about gender. Their research is aimed at finding a way to influence those inner states.

Large numbers of studies, however, have taken the sole point of view of the teacher. It is the teacher, it is assumed, who possesses power within the classroom. Because the concomitant of power is responsibility, it is also the teacher who is responsible for what happens in the classroom. This is certainly the perspective of the literature of recent educational reform. The teacher is powerful, the teacher is responsible, and the most effective way to facilitate educational change is by changing the teacher. Such change may be effected through motivation, through evaluation, or through training, but it is assumed that if the teacher changes, the outcomes of education will also change.

What this study proposes is an understanding of power that makes it relational, that locates it among the participants in the classroom. This would suggest to educational researchers that looking at teachers as the source of classroom power is an inadequate approach, and needs to be supplanted by more studies looking at the interaction among students and teachers in the enclosed space of the classroom.

* * *

The definition of power relations proposed here, that they are a "What Teachers and Students Can Do Here" structure, endows them with the potential to be a central concept in understanding what happens in classrooms. Teachers, teacher educators, and educational researchers alike might benefit by considering this way of understanding classroom interaction.

Appendix

Exploring Ideas About Power
Relations in Classrooms

ဢ ◆ ങ

For readers who seek to add depth and context to the ideas in this book, here is a bibliography of books and articles relevant to many of the issues that have been raised.

I: WHAT IS POWER?

A. Definitions, Explorations, Critiques

- Barnes, B. (1988). *The nature of power*. Cambridge, England: Polity Press.

Barnes believes that people use the concept of power to make moral judgments of other's actions. We claim that people can control both their own actions and those of others so that we can hold them responsible. This idea is exactly the one that saddles teachers with total responsibility for what happens in their classrooms. Barnes considers it a convenient falsehood.

He suggests that our belief that power is real is based on our recognition that we can affect the actions of others. We connect power too closely with the possession of coercive resources, and need to expand our understanding of the sources of power. Barnes holds that knowledge is a key source of power.

- Bell, R., & Harper, L. (1977). *Child effects on adults*. Lincoln: University of Nebraska Press.

This book from the literature of human development explores the interactive construction of child–adult interactions. Rather than seeing young children as the malleable recipients of adult influences, it places them as equal participants in shaping the behavior of their caregivers, just as their caregivers shape them.

- Boulding, K. (1989). *Three faces of power*. Newbury Park, CA: Sage.

Clear analysis of the sources and uses of power. Categories include threat power (the power to destroy, or the stick); economic power (the power to reward, or the carrot); and integrative power (the power to create positive relationships, or the hug).

- Etzioni, A. (1961). *Complex organizations: On power, involvement, and their correlates*. New York: The Free Press.

Similarly to Boulding, Etzioni defines power as coercive power, based on threats or on force; utilitarian, based on the promise of remuneration for compliance; and normative power, based on moral demands, which can involve either symbolic or social rewards for compliance.

- Fardon, R. (Ed.). (1985). *Power and knowledge: Anthropological and sociological approaches*. Edinburgh: Scottish Academic Press.

A key point made by Fardon is that "Power as such is never directly visible; it has to be read off" (p. 8). When we see that some people do what others want them to or that some people are able to do as they please despite the wishes of others, we say that we see power working. Yet, all we can really see is people acting; power is only the explanation we give for those actions.

- Foucault, M. (1980). *Power/knowledge: Selected interviews and other writings (1972–1977)*. New York: Pantheon.

No late-20th-century discussion of power relations would be complete without reference to this student of the workings of power in the world. His idea of power as a web of interactions within which humans live underlies the analysis of power relations in this book.

- Hall, P. (1985). Asymmetric relationships and the process of power. In H. Farberman & R. Perinbanayagam (Eds.), *Foundations of interpretive sociology: Original essays in symbolic interaction* (pp. 309–344). Greenwich, CT: JAI.

This symbolic interactionist claims that the powerful exercise their power when they create the context of their relationship with the powerless, defining its "values, meanings, social definitions, constructions of reality," setting the "rules of the game" (pp. 314–317). He views this task of context creation as being exclusive to the powerful.

- Lukes, S. (1974). *Power: A radical view.* London: MacMillan.

Lukes classifies ways of understanding power as one, two, and three dimensional. The one-dimensional view focuses on behavior, decision making, overt conflict, and the interests of individuals as revealed in their policy preferences; it ignores hidden aspects of power. The two-dimensional view considers both decision making and nondecision making, both overt and covert conflicts; it is too individualistic, and assumes that those unaware of their grievances are not oppressed. The three-dimensional view of power considers both decision making and control over the agenda of decisions to be made, and brings up latent and potential conflicts. It asks how people's perceptions are shaped to avoid their calling issues into question. Lukes defines power as latent or active, covert or overt, visible or invisible.

He interestingly points out that the two most common ways for social scientists to find out who has power has been to look at the results of controversy and assume that whoever wins must have power, and to ask people who they believe is powerful. Both methods testify to the impossibility of observing power directly.

- March, J. (1966). The power of power. In D. Easton (Ed.), *Varieties of political theory* (pp. 39–70). Englewood Cliffs, NJ: Prentice-Hall.

March, a theorist of interaction, criticizes the use of the concept of power to explain residual variance in outcomes; he says that when other ways of explaining what is happening fail, we turn to power as an explanation, even though we have no direct evidence that it is operating. He concludes that, "On the whole, ... power is a disappointing concept" (p. 70).

- Mishler, E. (1976). Skinnerism: Materialism minus the dialectic. *Journal for the Theory of Social Behavior, 6,* 21–47.

Mishler strongly critiques the extent to which behaviorist concepts support dualistic approaches to social control, tending to establish a technocratic elite of agents and a subclass of objectified persons. Thus he both illustrates and argues against the notion that people are either powerful or powerless, instead taking a more interactive perspective. This critique is significant in the context of education because of the strong influence of behaviorist theory on classroom management.

- Parenti, M. (1978). *Power and the powerless*. New York: St. Martin's Press.

Parenti's analysis of power looks closely at the effect of power on those described as the powerless. He raises the idea of a collusive relationship between those who have power and those whom they support or protect with that power, and for whom the loss of protecting or supporting power means a worsening of life conditions.

- Weber, M. (1947). *The theory of social and economic organization*. New York: Oxford University Press.

This classic sociological work includes an influential analysis of the sources of power. These sources are said to include charismatic authority, or the personal qualities of the individual; traditional authority, or the established mores of the society; and legal authority, or the office held by the individual. Thus, teachers might have authority based on their personalities, the respect that society has traditionally accorded to teachers, or the support the educational institution gives them in their roles.

- Wrong, D. (1979). *Power: Its forms, bases and uses*. New York: Harper & Row.

Wrong provides a clear and helpful summary of the history of traditional thought about power; his book is recommended for an overview of the concept.

B. Feminist and Social Activist Analysis of Power Relations

- Follett, M. P. (1918). *The new state: Group organization, the solution of popular government*. New York: Longman.

- Follett, M. P. (1924). *Creative experience*. New York: Longman.

- Follett, M. P. (1942). *Dynamic administration*. New York: Harper & Row.

Mary Parker Follett, whose work was highlighted by the late Seth Kreisberg, was an early proponent of interactive understanding of power relations. She believed that individuals operated in society, not for their own benefit or the benefit of others, but for the benefit of the whole society, and that power was necessarily a socially constructed aspect of group life. Her taken-for-granted feminism, mentioned only occasionally in the pages of these books, would be understood today as the essence of her ideas. She eliminated the concept of weak or powerless individuals from her thinking about power when she insisted that power was essentially collaborative.

- Janeway, E. (1980). *Powers of the weak*. New York: Knopf.

Janeway, a feminist scholar, explores how the very real powers of the othered—women, people of color, people of developing countries—are ignored, denigrated, and defined as not-really-power. Her critique of the traditional understanding of power locates it between the members of a relationship, while recognizing the interest of the strong in claiming power as their own. Their control of power gives the strong both credit and responsibility for the good and bad results of their actions because the weak do not contribute to what occurs. In fact, power is considered dangerous, and it is believed that the weak should not want it because it is harmful and corrupting.

In this view, if those who are ruled rebel, their rebellion is understood not as an exercise of their power, but as a problem of the powerful, to be dealt with rationally and responsibly, as one would deal with an earthquake. Rights (but not power) may be allocated to the weak; respect for these rights becomes the ethical duty of the powerful, but in crisis such rights may be abrogated. Janeway does not claim that this domination and subordination are not real, but rather that they are not the whole story about power. The weak do participate in the interactive reality that is power.

- Jaquette, J. (1984). Power as ideology: A feminist analysis. In J. Stiehm (Ed.), *Women's views of the political world of men* (pp. 7–30). Dobbs Ferry, NY: Transnational Publishers.

Jaquette's analysis of power suggests that forms of power such as persuasion and manipulation may be most accessible to the traditionally powerless, either for practical reasons or because deeply held cultural beliefs prevent them from considering the use of stronger forms of power. The resources they have to exert power may be so different from those of the traditionally powerful that observers (or even participants) have difficulty in seeing their use as involving power.

- Kreisberg, S. (1992). *Transforming power: Domination, empowerment, and education*. Albany, NY: SUNY Press.

Kreisberg, an educational activist, built on the ideas of Mary Parker Follett to develop a notion of shared power, or "power with." His pragmatic approach focused on the practical success and human advantages of a cooperative use of power.

- Lipman-Blumen, J. (1984). *Gender roles and power*. Englewood Cliffs, NJ: Prentice-Hall.

Some of the specifics of the "powers of the weak" are identified by Lipman-Blumen. She says that the more powerful use "macromanipulation" to control the less powerful; the less powerful can only use "micromanipulation, using intelligence, canniness, intuition, interpersonal skill, charm, sexuality, deception, and avoidance to offset the control of the powerful" (p. 8).

- Sharp, G. (1973). *The politics of nonviolent action*. Boston: P. Sargent Publishers.

Sharp gives a similar analysis in the political arena. He says power can be seen either as a function of government that affects the people, leaves them dependent on the government, and emanates from a few actors, or as constantly being created by individual actors in individual relationships in all parts of society, so that it is the government that depends on the peoples' actions.

II. ANALYSIS OF POWER RELATIONS IN CLASSROOMS

A. Traditional Approaches to Power Relations

- Grambs, J. (1957). The roles of the teacher. In L. Stiles (Ed.), *The teacher's role in American society* (pp. 73–93). New York: Harper & Row.

Grambs finds the sources of teachers' power in the various roles assigned to them. They are judges of achievement and evaluators of performance; they are experts, "the person who knows"; they keep discipline, maintaining the rules of the institution; they are receivers of confidences and dispensers of advice; and they are responsible for creating the moral atmosphere in the classroom. In enacting each of these roles, teachers assert and enact their power.

- Jackson, P. (1976). *Life in classrooms*. Chicago: University of Chicago Press.

Jackson, in his classic book, stresses the inequality of power between teachers and students. He assumes that teachers have power in the classroom simply because the students have to be there. At several points, he refers to them as being more like prisoners, constrained by physical force, than like factory workers, constrained by economic force. Therefore, he says, students indulge in such degrading practices as currying favor with the teacher by offering false compliments, "being helpful," and attempting to hide from the teacher words and actions that might be displeasing. Students are forced to comply with the wishes of the teacher just as they would with the wishes of a parent—even though they lack strong emotional ties with the teacher. Jackson finds the center of the teacher's authority in the ability to demand the student's attention.

- McNeil, L. (1982). *Contradictions of control: The organizational control of school knowledge.* Madison: Wisconsin Center for Public Policy.

McNeil, in seeking to understand how high school students' access to knowledge about economics is controlled by teachers, locates teachers' power in their choice of instructional methods and classroom styles.

- Noblit, G. (1993). Power and caring. *American Educational Research Journal, 30,* 23–38.

In his analysis of his experience in the classroom of a traditional African-American teacher who used teaching methods he initially disapproved of but came to appreciate, Noblit explores how her explicit use of teacher power could amount to caring for her students. His position with respect to classroom power is clear; for him, the teacher "is in charge of what her children do."

- Sarason, S. (1990). *The predictable failure of educational reform: Can we change course before it's too late?* San Francisco: Jossey-Bass.

Sarason has a traditional view of power, arguing in terms almost identical to those of Waller that the establishment of a teacher's power is "central to how they and others judge professional competence" (p. 80). This comment follows his reporting of complete agreement among a group of new teachers and their mentors that establishing power is a teacher's most important task.

- Sedlak, M., Wheeler, C., Pullin, D., & Cusick, P. (1986). *Selling students short: Classroom bargains and academic reform in the American high school.* New York: Teachers College Press.

These authors recognize that teachers are dependent on students for their feelings of "success, accomplishment, and satisfaction" in their jobs, and that teachers "must come to terms with students' definition of knowledge" (p. 99). Ideally, the teacher should be able to overcome the students' resistance to learning and engage them fully in the learning process. In reality, students and teachers often compromise, and their created compromises value human relations between teachers and students more highly than teaching and learning. Thus, students use the weapon of their attention to and approval of the teacher as they seek to reduce requirements for their classes and postpone any work that is expected of them, and "receive the highest grades they could for the least amount of effort" (p. 101).

- Sizer, T. (1984). *Horace's compromise: The dilemma of the American high school.* Boston: Houghton Mifflin.

Sizer describes students and teachers as making a more or less overt bargain intended to reduce discomfort for both. Students are thought to be unwilling to work, to learn, to experience stress. Teachers, on the other hand, want most of all to have classrooms that appear to be calm and under control, thus avoiding criticism from fellow teachers and administrators. According to Sizer, they bring their interests together in a mutual agreement ("Horace's Compromise") that the teachers will not demand much effort and the students will keep their behavior acceptable.

- Stubbs, M. (1983). *Language, schools and classrooms* (2nd ed.). London: Methuen.

Stubbs suggests that teacher power is found in the unequal division of conversational rights in the classroom. Teachers control the content, the amount, and the channels of talk. Teachers can not only control the amount of time they themselves will wait to respond to a student comment or question, but also can control the amount of time that a student has in which to respond to the teacher's comment or question. In order to have an answer recognized as "correct," a student must accept the teacher's right to organize instruction in the classroom, to choose the topic of discourse, and to evaluate answers.

- Waller, W. (1965). *The sociology of teaching.* New York: Wiley. (Original work published 1932)

In his chapter "Teaching as Institutionalized Leadership," Waller finds that power inheres in the teacher, is best exercised through the assertion of legitimate, or status-based, authority, and cannot be shared with students; if they have power it is an indication of the weakness and incompetence of the teacher. He speaks of the human desire to be dependent, to have decisions made for one, but recognizes student resistance to teacher control. The teacher must have his wishes carried out, if possible, "without a direct clash of wills between teacher and student" (p. 203). Yet, coercion has its place, and "the chief utility of anger seems to be in the transmission of taboos" (p. 305).

For Waller, the ideal is to establish a permanent and unshakable power structure in the classroom. It is the teacher's expectations that are at issue, not the students'. The well-behaved child simply accedes to the teacher's power; the misbehaving child attempts to resist it.

B. Analysis From the Point of View of "Classroom Management"

- Brophy, J. (1983). Classroom organization and management. *Elementary School Journal, 83,* 265–285.

Brophy, writing 50 years after Waller, describes the smoothly functioning classroom as one in which seemingly automatic orderly behavior is displayed by the students; devoting time to management or control is seen as an indicator of poor teaching.

- Duke, D. (Ed.). (1982). *Helping teachers manage classrooms.* Alexandria, VA: Association for Supervision and Curriculum Development.

Duke's discussion of classroom management, including discipline, behavior problems, classroom organization, student compliance, student accountability, control structures, control organization, and group management, leaves no room for the possibility of seeing teacher and students as jointly or interactively using or constructing power. The one-way quality of power is assumed. For example, student accountability means that the teacher is responsible for checking to be sure that the students are really complying with his or her demands.

- Lemlech, J. (1988). *Classroom management: Methods and techniques for elementary and secondary teachers* (2nd ed.). New York: Longman.

Lemlech gives an amazingly extensive list of teacher responsibilities:

Organize procedures and resources;
Arrange the environment to maximize efficiency;
Anticipate potential problems;
Set classroom routines and standards and communicate these to students;
Monitor compliance with standards and rules by teaching and reinforcing them, helping students to accept and understand them;
Preplan instruction, anticipating students' needs for materials, assistance, and movement;
Analyze tasks and learning experiences to anticipate time allotment, involvement, and task constraints;
Model appropriate social behavior;
Plan situations in which students will work together to achieve a common goal;
Teach interpersonal skills;
Ensure that students are successful in their group work;

Individualize and personalize instruction;
Give students opportunities to move around the classroom;
Check students' understanding of assignmnet instructions and of work in progress;
Verify students' short- and long-term accomplishments:
Check up on student behavior. (pp. 3–19)

Clearly, the teacher who can affect all this is assumed to have enormous power in the classroom.

- Manke, M. (1993). The sentimental image of the rural teacher. In P. Joseph & G. Burnaford (Eds.), *Images of schoolteachers in twentieth century America* (pp. 243–257). New York: St. Martin's Press.

This chapter describes incidents of teacher discipline through physical force and the textbooks that armed teachers with beliefs supporting their control of classrooms. It undercuts the idea that in previous times students were more compliant than they are today.

- Morine-Dershimer, G. (1985). *Talking, listening, and learning in elementary classrooms*. New York: Longman.

Morine-Dershimer finds that teachers who devote even 1% or 2% of their utterances to calls for attention are less effective than those who never need to seek control verbally. Thus, any time given to negotiation with students around issues of classroom power is seen as subtracting from student learning.

C. Interactive Approaches to Classroom Power

- Davies, B. (1982). *Life in the classroom and playground: The accounts of primary school children*. Boston: Routledge & Kegan Paul.

Davies, working in Australia, studied young children and their relationships with teachers. She saw some teachers handing over "responsibility for their agendas" (p. 116) in part to children, and the children finding ways to know in what areas they could act freely and in what areas the teacher's agenda was still firmly in place. Davies couched her analysis in terms of a teacher agenda of education and socialization, and a student agenda arising from the culture of childhood.

- Delamont, S. (1983). *Interaction in the classroom*. London: Methuen.

Delamont speaks of "bargaining" as an essential element of teacher–student interaction, although she does not appear to be referring to overt negotiation, but to a more subtle kind of interchange. Despite her recognition of the teacher's strong position—"Discussions about punishment in schools always turn on what sanctions teachers should be allowed; their right to *some* power over pupil's behavior is not questioned" (p. 57)—she also acknowledges student power, based primarily on the numerical dominance of pupils in the classroom, an essential and unchanging fact of classroom life. In her view, students attempt to determine what the teacher wants and to discover whether or not the teacher's goals are consonant with their own. Thus, whether they cooperate with the teacher or not, they are doing so for their own reasons and in their own interests. If they are disruptive, it is because they do not perceive a payoff in cooperation.

- Edwards, D., & Mercer, N. (1992). *Common knowledge: The development of understanding in the classroom.* New York: Routledge.

Edwards and Mercer studied closely the actions of teachers and students in settings where "progressive" methods, including small-group learning, were being used. They observed that even though students seemed to be working and speaking quite independently of the teacher, the teacher in fact had substantial control over topics, outcomes, and the direction in which discussion or exploration took place.

- Erickson, F., & Mohatt, G. (1982). Cultural organization of participation structures in two classrooms of Indian students. In G. Spindler (Ed.), *Doing the ethnography of schooling.* New York: Holt, Rinehart & Winston.

Erickson and Mohatt compare two classrooms with Native-American students, one with a Native-American teacher with extended experience in the school, the other with a White teacher with experience only in non-Native-American classrooms. They demonstrate how, in the course of the school year, the Native-American students, through their actions, brought the new teacher more and more in line with their cultural values. These included their desire that no person control the actions of any other, their desire that no person be singled out from the group for public performance or evaluation, and their preference with respect to the tempo of classroom events. In each respect, Erickson and Mohatt show what kinds of student actions led to the changes they document in the teacher's actions.

- Evertson, C., & Mehan, H. (1978). *Ecology of teaching.* San Francisco: Far West Laboratory for Educational Research and Development.

Evertson and Mehan, in a report that brought together their differing areas of expertise, wrote that "students control more of the interaction in the classroom than researchers previously thought was the case" (p. 7). They called for investigation of the processes through which this control is exerted and of the constraints operating on teachers in their classrooms (including those coming from students), and suggested that students and teachers all bring concerns to classrooms, and that if the concerns of the students are not dealt with, they will tend to "take over" the classroom.

- Furlong, V. (1971). Anancy goes to school: A case study of pupils' knowledge of their teachers. In S. Woods & M. Hammersley (Eds.), *School experience*. New York: St. Martin's Press.

Furlong, who studied children of Caribbean origin going to school in England, believes that students' power is based in the cultural values they bring to school. When these values are in tune with those presented by the school and the teacher, student power is quiescent; when these values are in conflict, students use their power by "mucking about." Her conclusion lends support to the ideas of Willis and Wallace, mentioned earlier.

- Gore, J. (1995). Foucault's poststructuralism and observational education research. In R. Smith & P. Wexler (Eds.), *Education, politics and identity: A study of power relations* (pp. 98–111). London: Falmer.

Gore's poststructuralist analysis of power relations in classrooms and other interactive sites is based on her close observation of student and teacher actions and discourse choices.

- Hausfather, S. (1996, April). *Power relations underlying the changing of conceptions of knowledge in an elementary classroom.* Paper presented at the annual meetings of the American Educational Research Association, New York.

This classroom teacher (now professor) engaged in self-study of his power-related thoughts and actions as he tried to share authority with students in his fifth-grade classroom in the interest of shifting his and their understanding of what knowledge is from a traditional to a more progressive and interactive concept. He focuses on the deep uneasiness he felt as he opened space in his classroom for students to participate overtly in building power relations.

- Hustler, D., & Payne, G. (1982). Power in the classroom. *Research in Education, 28,* 49–64.

Hustler and Payne, as part of a larger discussion of interactive power relations in the classroom, raise the question of the connection between the interactional and the institutional role of the teacher. They write:

Everyone knows that society delegates power and authority to teachers, and that in a classroom it is the teacher who has the power and the pupils who are subordinated parties in the teacher-pupil relationship .... How do a teacher and a class of pupils provide for that commonly known characteristic of the world through what they do in the typical lesson? (p. 54)

That is, the well-known institutional role of the teacher becomes an item that must be accounted for in the interactive construction of classroom reality, specifically, the power relations in the classroom. This is a strong example of research that is willing to pursue the notion of interactivity across the boundary of the taken-for-granted, and to incorporate and reanalyze traditional notions about classroom power.

They also locate much of the interaction around power in the classroom in the question of the ownership of classroom time. The teacher claims ownership of the time itself; students strive to assert control of it. They point out that the teacher's effort to make her control invisible (as advocated by students of classroom management) is really an effort to make it unchallengeable. The teacher strives to eliminate moments at which students might exercise power.

- Jones, A. (1989). The cultural production of classroom practice. *British Journal of Sociology, 10*, 19–31.

Jones, in her analysis of knowledge and control in two New Zealand classrooms, suggests that student power in the classroom extends into control of knowledge presented and studied and of teaching techniques. Her analysis is from the point of view of cultural reproduction, and she finds that the classroom in which students are of lower socioeconomic status is strongly influenced by the students' view of the proper way of learning and the proper content of learning.

They resist, using a variety of techniques, the efforts of the teacher to teach other material than memorizable facts, to use other methods than lecture and testing on notes, and to introduce any creative element or any input from themselves into the classroom. They succeed so well in this resistance that they do not practice or master the skills necessary for success on leaving examinations, which are not simply tests of memorizable facts; the teacher makes considerable efforts to counteract their resistance, but without success. Thus, student control of areas often considered sacrosanct to the teacher is demonstrated.

- Lampert, M. (1985). How do teachers manage to teach? Perspectives on problems in practice. *Harvard Educational Review, 55*, 178–194.

Lampert describes her own practice in the classroom. She exercises her power through her proximity to the student in question, and through such nonverbal markers as "a cool stare" or a touch on the shoulder. She knows that she could avoid exercising power, but that would be at the cost of "a chaotic classroom," which she does not wish to have. She solves her problem of controlling simultaneously the behavior of the children and the gender fairness of her own teaching by rearranging the room and regrouping the students for instruction.

- Metz, M. (1978). Clashes in the classroom: The importance of norms for authority. *Education and Urban Society, 11,* 13–47.

Metz observed teachers being required by high-track students to explain academic decisions, such as grades, the content of tests, the right answers to questions, and by low-track students to explain the punishments and sanctions they used. She concludes that the need to provide these explanations affected teachers' decision making. Sometimes it was easier for the teacher not to do something than to do it and then have to explain it.

- Metz, M. (1990). How social class differences shape teachers' work. In M. McLaughlin, J. Talbert, & N. Bascia (Eds.), *The contexts of teaching in secondary schools: Teachers' realities* (pp. 40–107). New York: Teachers College Press.

Metz saw students negotiating for and establishing a practice of leaving the last half of a period as a time to do homework—and in fact using the time for social conversation. Like Sedlak and Sizer, she concluded that teachers were trading student learning for positive social relations with students.

- Oyler, C. (1996). *Making room for students: Sharing teacher authority in room 106.* New York: Teachers College Press.

Oyler studied the sharing of authority in an urban first-grade classroom. Her observations of students and teacher in this classroom are full of instances of students shaping the teachers' actions and decisions. They are seen asking the teacher to talk about a particular topic, demanding time to write in journals, asserting their authority over the use of materials, and even insisting that desks be arranged in a particular way for journal-writing time. Although the teacher's intention was to share authority with the students, she had some qualms about the way they used it, but at the same time saw its positive effects on learning as strong enough to justify her risk taking.

- Pauly, E. (1991). *The classroom crucible: What really works, what doesn't, and why.* New York: Basic Books.

Pauly writes, "In the remarkable and fascinating form of power that exists in classrooms, everyone has power, and each person is subject to it; that is, every person in the classroom is partly controlled by the people he/she aims to control" (p. 57). His analysis of classroom power is based on this recognition, and is similar to the one discussed in this book.

- Richmond, V., & McCroskey, J. (Eds.). (1992). *Power in the classroom: Communication, control and concern.* Hillsdale, NJ: Lawrence Erlbaum Associates.

This volume addresses issues of power in the college classroom from the point of view of educational psychology, but a number of the chapters reach conclusions similar to those found in this book about the sources and workings of power. For example, V. Richmond and K. D. Roach, the authors of a chapter entitled "Power in the classroom: Seminal studies" (pp. 47–66) write, " ... for teacher power to exist, it must be granted by the students. Although the legitimate title of 'teacher' and the adult status of the instructor may lend some initial power to the teacher, if students do not accept or consent to compliance with teacher directives the teacher actually has no power" (p. 58). The topic of *Student resistance to control* (P. Cairn & T. Plan, pp. 85–100) becomes a catalogue of interrupting, question-asking and comment making among college students—the kinds of discourse choices that are described in this book. Staten, in a chapter entitled "Teacher and student concern and classroom power and control" (pp. 159–176) writes, "A more dialectical and less functionalist perspective considers power and control as dynamic processes that are constructed and negotiated between teacher and students" (p. 173).

- Swidler, A. (1979). *Organization without authority: Dilemmas of social control in free schools.* Cambridge, MA: Harvard University Press.

Swidler provides a rich analysis of interaction in "free schools," where the schools themselves acknowledged and invited student participation in the development of power relations. Interestingly, she looks elsewhere than teacher control for explanations of the success or failure of both learning and social relationships in these schools.

- Wolcott, H. (1987). The teacher as enemy. In G. Spindler (Ed.), *Education and cultural process: Anthropological approaches* (pp. 136–150). Prospect Heights, IL: Waveland Press.

Wolcott draws on his own experience as teacher in a Kwakiutl village, where student power became palpable for him in the classroom. He was able to identify a wide variety of student behaviors as oppositional to the agenda he was pursuing in the classroom. He links their actions to their cultural context, to which he was a stranger.

D. Analysis of Student Resistance

- Alpert, B. (1991). Students' resistance in the classroom. *Anthropology and Education Quarterly, 22,* 350–366.

Alpert says that oppositional actions by students are "a common, legitimate mode of expression and reaction in the classroom" (p. 363). She makes a close distinction between the concepts of resistance and misbehavior, and traces their roots in the literatures of sociology and psychology. She is particularly interested in the subtle forms of resistance observed in middle-class classrooms.

- Dorr-Bremme, D. (1992, April). *Discourse and social identity in a kindergarten–first grade classroom.* Paper presented at the annual meetings of the American Educational Research Association, San Francisco.

Dorr-Bremme discusses resistance to teacher expectations on the part of first-grade students. He describes such resistance, not as student misbehavior, but as their natural response to less-than-ideal learning situations.

- Everhart, R. (1983). Classroom management, student opposition, and the labor process. In M. Apple & L. Weis (Eds.), *Ideology and practice in schooling* (pp. 169–192). Philadelphia: Temple University Press.

Everhart describes the oppositional behavior of students "as a form of learning in itself" (p. 170). He analyzes it in terms of the resistance found among assembly-line workers.

- Grahame, P., & Jardine, D. (1990). Deviance, resistance and play: A study in the communicative organization of trouble in the classroom. *Curriculum Inquiry, 20,* 283–304.

These authors analyze incidents of resistance to teacher agendas by lower class young men, and introduce the idea that playfulness is part of the youths' agenda in subverting the teacher's intentions.

- MacLeod, J. (1995). *Ain't no makin' it: Aspiration and attainment in a low-income neighborhood.* Boulder, CO: Westview Press.

MacLeod's analysis of resistance among two groups of low-income urban youths concludes that there is little difference in outcomes for those who resist the pressures brought to bear by school and society and those who do not.

- Pignatelli, F. (1994). *Valuing student refusal: Some considerations for school leaders and reformers.* Unpublished manuscript.

Pignatelli speaks of the "promise of transgressive acts" (p. 1), urging his readers to think of students' use of their power as boding well for their education.

- Trueba, H. (1989). *Raising silent voices: Educating linguistic minorities for the twenty-first century.* New York: Newbury House.

Trueba gives an excellent example of how student resistance to the teacher's claim to knowledge plays out in the classroom He describes a Sudanese boy in an American classroom, who was asked to locate the Mississippi River on a map. He sat silent, and then said, "It is indeed the largest American river, but I know the Nile and it is bigger." He continued to describe the Nile and its importance, but "the teacher pressed on with the subject of American rivers" (p. 73).

- Wallace, C. (1987). *For richer, for poorer: Growing up in and out of work.* London: Tavistock.

Wallace describes young people who have ideas about possibilities for their future lives that may or may not be furthered by the school. Their cooperation with teachers depends on the connection between what they believe they can get from the school and the plans they have made for themselves.

- Willis, P. (1977). *Learning to labour: How working class kids get working class jobs.* New York: Columbia University Press.

Willis describes the boys he observed as being convinced they do not want the kinds of jobs or the kinds of lifestyles for which school would prepare them, and therefore seeing no reason to cooperate with the goals of the school. Their view of those who do cooperate is that they are too stupid to see the superiority of the working-class lifestyle and are missing out on the good things in life.

III. ANALYSIS OF CLASSROOM LANGUAGE WITH RESPECT TO THE DETAILS OF CONSTRUCTING POWER RELATIONS

- Ballenger, C. (1992). Because you like us: The language of control. *Harvard Educational Review, 62,* 199–208.

Ballenger, a preschool teacher in a Haitian community in Massachusetts, describes how she learned to apply the relational and linguistic styles she saw among Haitian parents, teachers, and children. She tells how pleased and supportive the young children themselves were about her change in style.

- Barnes, D. (1992). *From communication to curriculum* (2nd. ed.). Portsmouth, NH: Boynton/Cook.

Barnes describes three ways that teachers cut off student talk—by not responding at all to what is said, by insisting that correct vocabulary be used, and by responding to grammatical form and not content. In that way, they are able to control student responses without challenging the validity of what the students are saying or the students' right to speak.

- Bossert, S. (1978). Classroom structure and teacher authority. *Education and Urban Society, 11*, 49–59.

Bossert observed a teacher who, whenever she wished to exert control over student behavior, offered verbal criticism of their failure to use Standard English in the classroom. For this teacher, offering criticism was a discourse strategy she used to assert her power.

- Carlsen, W. (1991). Questioning in classrooms: A sociolinguistic perspective. *Review of Educational Research, 61*, 157–178.

Carlsen offers a detailed analysis of the sociolinguistic perspective on questioning in classrooms, contrasting it with process–product research on the matter. He identifies the essence of the sociolinguistic point of view as the assumption that teacher questions are mutually generated by teachers and students, rather than by teachers alone.

- Cazden, C. (1988). *Classroom discourse: The language of teaching and learning.* Portsmouth, NH: Heinemann.

Cazden, conducting research in the first-grade classroom in which she was teaching, observed children forgetting the teacher's expectations, engaging in secret communications with their peers, exploring the limits of the teacher's rules, passing notes, reading or working on material the teacher had not provided, and laughing about outside matters. She guessed that oppositional behaviors like these have their own appeal to children, just as a matter of making their own choices in a setting where the teacher is director. She even discussed her fears, similar to those of student teacher Courtney Bridgestone (discussed in chaps. 3 and 9 of this book), that children would have more power than she did.

- Edwards, D., & Mercer, N. (1987). *Common knowledge: The development of understanding in the classroom.* London: Routledge.

Edwards and Mercer remark that under normal classroom circumstances, learners are unlikely to argue with the teachers' representation of the right answer (p. 156). Edwards and Mercer closely studied the actions of teachers and students in settings where progressive methods, including small-group learning, were being used. They observed that even though students seemed to be working and speaking quite independently of the teacher, the teacher had substantial control over topics, outcomes, and the direction in which discussion or exploration took place. They observed that students are unlikely to question teachers' formulations of "right" answers.

- Green, J., & Weade, R. (1985). Reading between the words: Social cues to lesson participation. *Theory Into Practice, 24,* 14–21.

Green and Weade, in a sociolinguistic analysis, locate teachers' power in classroom discourse; the teacher controls metamessages in the classroom. The teacher determines who can talk, when someone can talk, where someone can talk, about what subject talk is permitted, to whom someone can talk, and in what ways someone can talk. In addition, the teacher is the source of the messages that tell the students what the activity at hand is, "what we are doing."

- Griffin, P., & Mehan, H. (1981). Sense and ritual in classroom discourse. In F. Coulmas (Ed.), *Conversational routine: Explorations in standardized communication situations and prepatterned speech* (pp. 187–213). Hague, The Netherlands: Mouton.

Griffin and Mehan base their discussion on the concept of the teacher's expected control of the turn-allocation procedure in the classroom, an assumption underlying Mehan's *Learning Lessons.* Considering how students might learn to manipulate this control, they describe how "as the year progressed students became adept at locating the seams in lesson [teacher] discourse .... Students effectively gained control of the floor." He and Griffin did not consider the possibility of understanding the lesson presented by the teacher as existing in the seams of student discourse, but from an interactive point of view, either interpretation is possible.

- McDermott, R. (1977). The ethnography of speaking and reading. In R. Shuy (Ed.), *Linguistic theory: What can it say about reading?* (pp. 153–185). Newark, DE: International Reading Association.

McDermott bases his research on the assumption that the actions and interactions of teacher and students are always creating the environment in which they continue to interact. This environment can only be understood through the study of minute details of action; any effort to alter the environment would have to come through the alteration of these minute details.

In this article, McDermott considers classroom power relations. "Teaching," he says, "is invariably a form of coercion" (p. 156). This inevitable coercion of students can be rendered harmful or harmless according to the actions and interactions of student and teacher.

He analyzes turn taking as part of the power relationship. In a classroom situation, the teacher has an institutional right to assign turns in conversation; the nature of power relationships depends in part on whether the teacher does in fact allocate all turns and what rules govern students' acquisition of turns.

- Mehan, H. (1979). *Learning lessons*. Cambridge, MA: Harvard University Press.

Mehan developed the Initiation–Response–Evaluation model for understanding discourse in classrooms. The teacher wraps her control around the student response as she both elicits and evaluates it. Thus, the teacher decides when to begin an interaction (and thus, when a response is appropriate), and when to end an interaction (or pass on to another one). At the same time, the teacher determines in the evaluation whether the response is acceptable. Courtney Cazden, who was the teacher he was observing, later wrote, "Where the researcher sees order, I often felt impending chaos" (Cazden, 1988, p. 44). When Mehan lists the interruptions in the teacher's day that lead her to focus on "keeping the lid on," "just maintaining," and "getting through the day," the actions of children are not included.

- Mercer, N. (1995). *The guided construction of knowledge: Talk amongst teachers and learners*. Philadelphia: Multilingual Matters.

Mercer studied closely the interactive strategies used by teachers in guiding the construction of knowledge. He is acutely aware of the tension progressive teachers experience between their sense that student freedom in learning is highly productive and their concern that students construct knowledge in ways that relate to the school curriculum. His is an uncompromising analysis of the ethnomethodology that prevails in classrooms.

- Mishler, E. (1972). Implications of teacher strategies for language and cognition: Observations in first-grade classrooms. In C. Cazden, V. John, & D. Hymes (Eds.), *Functions of language in the classroom* (pp. 267–298). New York: Teachers College Press.

Mishler explores the effects of teachers' discourse choices on learning and classroom context. He observed teachers using both direct and indirect discourse in talking with students, and concluded that indirect discourse was a feature of good teaching.

- Phillips, S. (1983). *The invisible culture: Communication in classroom and community on the Warm Springs Indian Reservation.* New York: Longman.

Phillips describes the way Native-American students express their culture through their power-related actions in classrooms. She sees their power being exercised through their willingness or unwillingness to accept, or ratify, the teacher's statements of the teacher. A sociolinguist, she points out that persons engaging in interactions must ratify the utterances of others, claiming them as understandable and appropriate; to fail to do this is a significant action and a use of power.

- Puro, P., & Bloome. D. (1987). Understanding classroom communication. *Theory into Practice, 26,* 26–31.

Puro and Bloome see the teacher as exercising power in an interactional context both through words and through nonverbal means such as silence, behavior, action, and even the physical arrangements of the room. Even when the teacher does not state what the rules are, they believe, what the teacher accepts is the criterion for students of what is appropriate. They are dependent on the teacher even for the definition of the situation in which they must live.

IV. ANALYTICAL TOOLS FOR UNDERSTANDING CLASSROOM POWER RELATIONS

A. Study of Human Kinetic Behavior

- Birdwhistell, R. (1970). *Kinesics and context.* Philadelphia: University of Pennsylvania Press.

- Scheflen, A. (1974). *How behavior means.* New York: Anchor.

These are two foundational works in the understanding of how the movements and positioning of the human body affect communication. Going far beyond what is usually thought of as "body language," they offer a detailed analysis of communicative actions that most often play out at an unconscious level, but are full of meaning and strongly affect communicative interaction. McDermott (1978) calls this "torso, elbow, and vocal chord work" (p. 323).

B. Conversational Analysis

- Sacks, H., Schegloff, E., & Jefferson, G. (1974). A simplest systematics for the organization of turn-taking in conversation. *Language, 50,* 696–735.

This classic article, coauthored by three leading conversational analysts, exemplifies the study of minute details of conversational interaction. As with the kinetic analysis of Birdwhistell and Scheflen, such details are not produced consciously, yet are essential to our understanding of the meaning of others' communications.

C. Ethnomethodology

- Garfinkel, H. (1967). *Studies in ethnomethodology.* Englewood Cliffs, NJ: Prentice-Hall.

Garfinkel, a sociologist, originated the study of the rules people use in interaction. Unlike the explicit rules that may be verbalized by participants or laid down in etiquette books, these rules are created through interaction and adhered to because they make communication and smooth interaction possible.

D. Microethnography

- McDermott, R., & Roth, D. (1978). The social organization of behavior: Interactional approaches. *Annual Review of Anthropology, 7,* 321–45.

- McDermott, R., & Tylbor, H. (1986). On the necessity of collusion in conversation. In S. Fisher & A. Todd (Eds.), *Discourse and institutional authority: Medicine, education, and law* (pp. 123–139). Norwood, NJ: Ablex.

Microethnographers study human interaction in minute detail, using kinesics, conversational analysis, and ethnomethodology as tools. Most often they work from videotapes of interaction, expending great effort just to see the details and patterns of interaction that have been recorded, and then analyzing them exhaustively.

McDermott criticizes some sociologists as claiming to study interaction while not looking at real interactions. He says they have defined roles for people—gender roles, ethnic roles, and institutional roles like "student" and "teacher"—and study the way the roles are enacted, rather than the actions of individual actors. The social order is then seen as consisting of the roles and their interactions.

McDermott, however, argues that the social order in fact consists of the context that individual actors create by their actions. This social order is consistent only in that it is always being constructed and affirmed by the actions of the individuals involved. Part of the material out of which they create the social order is certainly their understanding of their roles as previously defined and lived, but only part.

E. Studies of Discourse

- Brown, P., & Levinson, S. (1978). Universals in language usage: Politeness phenomena. In E. Goody (Ed.), *Questions and politeness: Strategies in social interaction*. Cambridge, England: Cambridge University Press.

Brown and Levinson introduce the concept of negative face, which can be understood as the ability to avoid being constrained by the power of others. "Face Threatening Acts" are those that suggest that constraints will be applied. Brown and Levinson hold that an important part of "politeness" consists of avoiding, limiting, or excusing face threatening acts toward other individuals. The extent to which a person feels required to "be polite" in this sense is a measure of the nature of the power relationship in which he or she is participating in the context under consideration. Thus, Brown and Levinson open up an understanding of the use of language as both a measure of perceived power and a way of displaying or exercising power.

- Fisher, S., & Todd, A. (Eds.). (1986). *Discourse and institutional authority: Medicine, education, and law.* Norwood, NJ: Ablex.

Several of the authors represented in Fisher and Todd's collection describe discourse strategies that contribute to the use of power. These include strategies related to the control of the topic (e.g., changing the subject or ignoring the efforts of other participants to introduce new topics), as well those involving ordinarily unacceptable usages such as extreme brevity and refusal to accept answers that have been offered.

- Fishman, P. (1983). Interaction: The work women do. In B. Thorne, C. Kramarae, & N. Henley (Eds.), *Language, gender and society* (pp. 89–101). Rowley, MA: Newbury House.

Fishman studied audio recordings of male–female couples alone in their homes, and found an unequal power relationship in their use of language. She suggests that power is a matter of "imposing one's definition of what is possible, what is right, what is rational, what is real." Insisting on the interactive nature of the power relationship, she refuses to view power as "an abstract force operating on people," but names it as "a human accomplishment, situated in everyday interaction" (p. 89).

She found males imposing through language their own definition of the relationships they participate in. They assume, and correctly, that conversations they begin and topics they raise will be pursued as long as they want to pursue them. Women, on the other hand, seem to perceive their own conversational overtures as tentative, subject to possible rejection—and they too are correct in their perceptions, according to Fishman's data. She concludes that women perform a disproportionate share of the work in initiating and maintaining conversations within relationships. She seems to assume that leisure is the lot of the powerful, while the enslaved powerless perform heavy conversational labor. A more interactive understanding of her materials, however, might suggest that the women are contributing to the development of the relationship through their labor with language. Thus, they participate actively from their position of weakness just as the men do from their position of strength.

- Grice, H. (1975). Logic and conversation. In P. Cole & J. Morgan (Eds.), *Syntax and semantics, 3, Speech acts* (pp. 41–58). Cambridge, MA: Harvard University Press.

In this classic of sociolinguistics, Grice develops the idea that whenever use of language deviates from the norm, there is a reason for the deviation, an intention or meaning that is being conveyed.

- Searle, J. (1966). *Speech acts: An essay in the philosophy of language.* New York: Cambridge University Press.

This philosopher–linguist unfolded the concept of *indirect speech acts.* These discourse choices may have one apparent meaning, whereas their actual weight in the conversation may be completely different.

References

⅓ ◆ ⅔

Alpert, B. (1991). Students' resistance in the classroom. *Anthropology and Education Quarterly, 22,* 350–366.

Apple, M. (1993). *Official knowledge.* New York: Routledge.

Apple, M. (1996). *Cultural politics and education.* New York: Teachers College Press.

Bateson, G. (1979). *Mind and nature: A necessary unity.* New York: Bantam.

Benedict, R. (1938). Continuities and discontinuities in cultural conditioning. *Psychiatry, 1,* 161–167.

Brophy, J. (1983). Classroom organization and management. *Elementary School Journal, 83,* 265–285.

Brown, P., & Levinson, S. (1978). Universals in language usage: Politeness phenomena. In E. Goody (Ed.), *Questions and politeness: Strategies in social interaction* (pp. 56–289). Cambridge, England: Cambridge University Press.

Bruner, J. (1966). *Toward a theory of instruction.* Cambridge, MA: Harvard University Press.

Byars, B. (1981). *The Cybil war.* New York: Viking.

Cangelosi J. (1988). *Classroom management strategies: Gaining and maintaining students' cooperation* (2nd ed.). New York: Longman.

Carle, E. (1989). *The very hungry caterpillar.* New York: Scholastic.

Carlsen, W. R. (1991). Questioning in classrooms: A sociolinguistic perspective. *Review of Educational Research, 61,* 157–178.

Carnoy, M. (1984). The dialectic of education: An alternative approach to education and social change in developing countries. In E. Gumbert (Ed.), *Expressions of power in education: Studies of class, gender and race* (pp. 9–27). Atlanta: Center for Cross-cultural Education.

Cazden, C. (1988). *Classroom discourse: The language of teaching and learning.* Portsmouth, NH: Heinemann.

Collier, J., & Collier, C. (1994). *My brother Sam is dead.* New York: Scholastic.

Delpit, L. (1988). The silenced dialogue: Power and pedagogy in educating other people's children. *Harvard Educational Review, 38,* 280–298.

Donaldson, M. (1978). *Children's minds.* New York: Norton.

Doyle, W. (1990). Classroom knowledge as a foundation for teaching. *Teachers College Record, 91,* 347–360.

Duke, D. (Ed.). (1982). *Helping teachers manage classrooms.* Alexandria, VA: Association for Supervision and Curriculum Development.

Fine, M. (1991). *Framing dropouts: Notes on the politics of an urban public high school.* Albany: State University of New York Press.

Finn, J. (1972). Expectations and the educational environment. *Review of Educational Research, 42*, 387–410.

Foucault, M. (1980). *Power/knowledge: Selected interviews and other writings (1972–1977)*. New York: Pantheon.

Fraatz, J. (1987). *The politics of reading: Power, opportunity and prospects for change in America's schools*. New York: Teacher's College Press.

Gadamer, H-G. (1976). *Philosophical hermeneutics* (D. Linge, Trans.). Berkeley: University of California Press.

Gamoran, A., & Dreeben, R. (1986). Coupling and control in educational organizations. *Administrative Science Quarterly, 31*, 612–632.

Geertz. C. (1973). *The interpretation of cultures*. New York: Bantam.

Gore, J. (1995). Foucault's poststructuralism and observational education research. In R. Smith & P. Wexler (Eds.), *Education, politics and identity: A study of power relations* (pp. 98–111). London: Falmer.

Grahame, P., & Jardine, D. (1990). Deviance, resistance and play: A study in the communicative organization of trouble in the classroom. *Curriculum Inquiry, 20*, 283–304.

Grice, H. (1975). Logic and conversation. In P. Cole & J. Morgan (Eds.), *Syntax and semantics, 3, Speech acts* (pp. 41–58). Cambridge, MA: Harvard University Press.

Griffin, P., & Mehan, H. (1981). Sense and ritual in classroom discourse. In F. Coulmas (Ed.), *Conversational routine: Explorations in standardized communication situations and prepatterned speech* (pp. 187–213). Hague, The Netherlands: Mouton.

Hustler, D., & Payne, G. (1982). Power in the classroom. *Research in education, 28*, 49–64.

Hynds, S. (1994). *Making connections*. Norwood, MA: Christopher-Gordon Publishers.

Janeway, E. (1980). *The powers of the weak*. New York: Knopf.

Jones, A. (1981). The cultural production of classroom practice. *British Journal of Sociology, 10*, 19–31.

Karabel, J., & Halsey, A. (Eds.). (1977). *Power and ideology in education*. Oxford, England: Oxford University Press.

Kohl, H. (1995). *I won't learn from you and other thoughts on creative maladjustment*. New York: New Press.

Kounin, J. (1970). *Discipline and group management in classrooms*. New York: Holt, Rinehart & Winston.

Lakoff, G., & Johnson, M. (1980). *Metaphors we live by*. Chicago: University of Chicago Press.

Lampert, M. (1985). How do teachers manage to teach? Perspectives on problems in practice. *Harvard Educational Review, 55*, 178–194.

MacLaren, P. (1988). *Life in schools: An introduction to critical pedagogy in the foundations of education*. New York: Longman.

McCormick, T., & Noriega, T. (1986). Low versus high expectations: A review of teacher expectations effects on minority students, *Journal of Educational Equity and Leadership, 6*, 224–234.

McDermott, R., & Roth, D. (1978). The social organization of behavior: Interactional approaches. *Annual Review of Anthropology, 7*, 321–345.

McDermott, R., & Tylbor, H. (1986). On the necessity of collusion in conversation. In S. Fisher & A. Todd (Eds.), *Discourse and institutional authority: Medicine, education and law* (pp. 123–139). Norwood, NJ: Ablex.

McNeil, L. (1982). *Contradictions of control: The organizational control of school knowledge*. Madison, WI: Wisconsin Center for Public Policy.

Mehan, H. (1979). *Learning lessons*. Cambridge, MA: Harvard University Press.

Metz, M. (1990). How social class differences shape teachers' work. In M. McLaughlin, J. Talbert, & N. Bascia (Eds.), *The contexts of teaching in secondary schools: Teachers' realities* (pp. 40–107). New York: Teachers College Press.

Mishler, E. (1972). Implications of teacher strategies for language and cognition: Observations in first-grade classrooms. In C. Cazden, V. John, & D. Hymes (Eds.), *Functions of language in the classroom* (pp. 267–298). New York: Teachers College Press.

Mishler, E. (1976). Skinnerism: Materialism minus the dialectic. *Journal for the Theory of Social Behavior, 6*, 21–47.

Modzierz, G., McConville, M., & Strauss, H. (1968). Classroom status and perceived performance in first-graders. *Journal of Social Psychology, 75*, 185–190.

Morine-Dershimer, G. (1985). *Talking, listening, and learning in elementary classrooms*. New York: Longman.

Noddings, N. (1991). Stories in dialogue: Caring and interpersonal reasoning. In C. Witherell & N. Noddings (Eds.), *Stories lives tell: Narrative and dialogue in education* (pp. 157–170). New York: Teachers College Press.

Noddings, N. (1995). Goal setting in education. In R. Miller (Ed.), *Educational freedom for a democratic society: A critique of national goals, standards and curriculum* (pp. 77–85). Brandon, VT: Resource Center for Redesigning Education.

Overhaul of teacher recruiting, training, rewards encouraged. (1996, September 13). *Mankato Free Press*, p. 3A.

Oyler, C. (1996). *Making room for students: Sharing teacher authority in room 106.* New York: Teachers College Press.

Rist, R. (1970). Student social class and teacher expectations: The self-fulfilling prophecy of ghetto education. *Harvard Educational Review, 40*, 411–451.

Sadker, M., & Sadker, D. (1994). *Failing at fairness: How America's schools cheat girls.* New York: Scribner's.

Sarason, S. (1990). *The predictable failure of educational reform: Can we change course before it's too late?* San Francisco: Jossey-Bass.

Searle, J. (1966). *Speech acts: An essay in the philosophy of language.* Cambridge, England: Cambridge University Press.

Sedlak, M., Wheeler, C., Pullin, D., & Cusick, P. (1986). *Selling students short: Classroom bargains and academic reform in the American high school.* New York: Teachers College Press.

Sizer, T. (1984). *Horace's compromise: The dilemma of the American high school.* Boston: Houghton Mifflin.

Speare, E. (1983). *The sign of the beaver.* Boston: Houghton Mifflin.

Spence, J. (1984). *The memory palace of Matteo Ricci.* New York: Viking Penguin.

Spinelli, J. (1990). *Maniac Magee.* New York: HarperCollins.

Swick, K. (1985). *Disruptive student behavior in the classroom.* Washington, DC: National Education Association.

Swidler, A. (1979). *Organization without authority: Dilemmas of social control in free schools.* Cambridge, MA: Harvard University Press.

Tyack, David B. (1974). *The one best system: A history of American urban education.* Cambridge, MA: Harvard University Press.

Vygotsky, L. (1986). *Thought and language.* Cambridge, MA: MIT Press.

Waller, W. (1965). *The sociology of teaching.* New York: Wiley. (Original work published 1932)

White, J.J. (1989). The power of politeness in the classroom: Cultural codes that create and constrain knowledge construction. *Journal of Curriculum and Supervision, 4*, 298–321.

Wolcott, H. (1987). The teacher as enemy. In G. Spindler (Ed.), *Education and cultural process: Anthropological approaches* (pp. 136–150). Prospect Heights, IL: Waveland Press.

Author Index

80 ◆ 03

Subject Index

❧ ◆ ❧